W9-AOU-669

A HISTORICAL READER

The Presidency

nextext

Compiled by: Ethel Wood, Princeton High School, Princeton, New Jersey

Cover: *George Washington,* from the engraving by W. Nutter, after C. G. Stuart. Courtesy Tony Stone Images.

Printed in the United States of America

ISBN 0-618-04821-9

1 2 3 4 5 6 7 — QKT — 06 05 04 03 02 01 00

Table of Contents

PART II: INTEREST GROUPS AND THE MEDIA

*Throughout the reader, vocabulary words appear in boldface
type and are footnoted. Specialized or technical words and
phrases appear in lightface type and are footnoted.*

A Changing
Balance of Power

"We Don't Propose to Establish Kings"

BY PAGE SMITH

The presidency was created by the writers of the Constitution in 1787. The Articles of Confederation had not provided for a President, and it was clear that such a government was too weak to be effective. However, the founders wanted to be sure the chief executive could not become too powerful. Benjamin Franklin proposed that the executive "shall receive no salary, stipend, fee, or reward whatsoever" for his services. In the following excerpt from his book, The Shaping of America, *historian Page Smith recounts Franklin's arguments, which reflect the founders' deep-seated fear of the President becoming a tyrant.*

. . .The Doctor[1] was convinced that there were "two passions which have a powerful influence on the affairs of men. These are ambition and avarice; the love of power, and the love of money. Separately each of these

---

[1] The Doctor—Benjamin Franklin.

has great force in prompting men to action; but when united in view of the same object, they have in many minds the most violent effects. Place before the eyes of such men, a post of honor that shall be at the same time a place of profit, and they will move heaven and earth to obtain it." Who, Franklin asked, would enter the lists for the office of chief executive under the new government? "It will not be the wise and moderate; the lovers of peace and good order, the men fittest for the trust. It will be the bold and violent, the men of strong passions and **indefatigable**[2] activity in their selfish pursuits. These will thrust themselves into your Government and be your rulers." While the chief executive might start out with a moderate salary, he would soon be busy to **augment**[3] it. Franklin continued: "All history informs us [that] there has been in every State & Kingdom a constant kind of warfare between the governing & the governed: the one striving to obtain more for its support, and the other to pay less. And this has occasioned great convulsions, actual civil wars. . . or enslaving of the people . . . . There is scarce a king in a hundred who would not, if he could, follow the example of Pharaoh, get first all the peoples' money, then all their lands, and then make them and their children servants for ever. It will be said, that we don't propose to establish Kings. I know it. But there is a natural inclination in mankind to kingly Government . . . . I am apprehensive therefore, perhaps too apprehensive, that the Government of these States, may in future times, end in a Monarchy. But this catastrophe I think may be long delayed, if in our proposed System we do not sow the seeds of contention, faction & **tumult**,[4] by making our posts of honor, places of profit."

---

[2] **indefatigable**—untiring.

[3] **augment**—increase; supplement.

[4] **tumult**—disturbance; commotion.

QUESTIONS TO CONSIDER

1. In your own words, how would you explain Benjamin Franklin's argument that the chief executive should receive no salary?

2. What does Franklin mean by "warfare between the governing and the governed"?

3. Do you agree with Franklin's recommendation to the convention? Why or why not?

Federalist Papers
(Number 69)

BY ALEXANDER HAMILTON AS "PUBLIUS"

The Constitution was signed on September 17, 1787. To take effect, it had to be ratified by at least nine of the thirteen states. By June 1788 the required nine states had ratified it, but without the support of the large states of New York and Virginia, everyone knew that the new Constitution would be meaningless. In an effort to convince the legislatures of these states to ratify, James Madison, Alexander Hamilton, and John Jay penned the famous Federalist Papers. *These documents represent the best explanation of American political philosophy in existence. In the* Federalist Papers *(Number 69), Alexander Hamilton—writing under the name "Publius"— defined "the real character of the executive." His arguments were meant to assure the New York legislature that the proposed presidency was a limited, democratic office—not a kingship like that of Great Britain. He stressed that the Constitution deliberately placed many restrictions on the power of the President.*

The Real Character of the Executive
From the New York Packet,
Friday, March 14, 1788.

To the People of the State of New York:

I PROCEED now to trace the real characters of the proposed Executive, as they are marked out in the plan of the convention. This will serve to place in a strong light the unfairness of the representations which have been made in regard to it.

The first thing which strikes our attention is, that the executive authority, with few exceptions, is to be vested in a single **magistrate**.[1] This will scarcely, however, be considered as a point upon which any comparison can be grounded; for if, in this particular, there be a resemblance to the king of Great Britain, there is not less a resemblance to the Grand Seignior, to the khan of Tartary, to the Man of the Seven Mountains, or to the governor of New York.

That magistrate is to be elected for FOUR years; and is to be re-eligible as often as the people of the United States shall think him worthy of their confidence. In these circumstances there is a total **dissimilitude**[2] between HIM and a king of Great Britain, who is an HEREDITARY monarch, possessing the crown as a **patrimony**[3] descendible to his heirs forever; but there is a close analogy between HIM and a governor of New York, who is elected for THREE years, and is re-eligible without limitation or intermission. If we consider how much less time would be requisite for establishing a dangerous influence in a single State, than for establishing a like influence throughout the United States, we must conclude that a duration of FOUR years for the

---

[1] **magistrate**—chief ruler, in this case the President.

[2] **dissimilitude**—difference.

[3] **patrimony**—inheritance from a father.

Chief Magistrate of the Union is a degree of permanency far less to be dreaded in that office, than a duration of THREE years for a corresponding office in a single State.

The President of the United States would be liable to be impeached, tried, and, upon conviction of treason, bribery, or other high crimes or **misdemeanors**,[4] removed from office; and would afterwards be liable to prosecution and punishment in the ordinary course of law. The person of the king of Great Britain is sacred and inviolable; there is no constitutional tribunal to which he is **amenable**;[5] no punishment to which he can be subjected without involving the crisis of a national revolution. In this delicate and important circumstance of personal responsibility, the President of Confederated America[6] would stand upon no better ground than a governor of New York, and upon worse ground than the governors of Maryland and Delaware.

The President of the United States is to have power to return a bill, which shall have passed the two branches of the legislature, for reconsideration; and the bill so returned is to become a law, if, upon that reconsideration, it be approved by two thirds of both houses. The king of Great Britain, on his part, has an absolute negative upon the acts of the two houses of Parliament. The disuse of that power for a considerable time past does not affect the reality of its existence; and is to be ascribed wholly to the crown's having found the means of substituting influence to authority, or the art of gaining a majority in one or the other of the two houses, to the necessity of exerting a **prerogative**[7] which could seldom be exerted without hazarding some degree of national

---

[4] **misdemeanors**—illegal acts.

[5] **amenable**—open to.

[6] Confederated America—At this time, Americans thought of the thirteen states almost as thirteen independent countries that had agreed to join together, or "confederate," to accomplish certain goals, like having a common foreign policy.

[7] **prerogative**—exclusive right.

agitation. The qualified negative of the President differs widely from this absolute negative of the British sovereign; and tallies exactly with the revisionary authority of the council of revision of this State, of which the governor is a constituent part. In this respect the power of the President would exceed that of the governor of New York, because the former would possess, singly, what the latter shares with the chancellor and judges; but it would be precisely the same with that of the governor of Massachusetts, whose constitution, as to this article, seems to have been the original from which the convention have copied.

The President is to be the "commander-in-chief of the army and navy of the United States," and of the militia of the several States, when called into the actual service of the United States. He is to have power to grant reprieves and pardons for offenses against the United States, EXCEPT IN CASES OF IMPEACHMENT; to recommend to the consideration of Congress such measures as he shall judge necessary and expedient; to convene, on extraordinary occasions, both houses of the legislature, or either of them, and, in case of disagreement between them WITH RESPECT TO THE TIME OF ADJOURNMENT, to adjourn them to such time as he shall think proper; to take care that the laws be faithfully executed; and to commission all officers of the United States." In most of these particulars, the power of the President will resemble equally that of the king of Great Britain and of the governor of New York. The most material points of difference are these: First. The President will have only the occasional command of such part of the militia of the nation as by legislative provision may be called into the actual service of the Union. The king of Great Britain and the governor of New York have at all times the entire command of all the militia within their several jurisdictions. In this article, therefore, the power of the President would be inferior to that of either the monarch or the governor. Secondly. The President is to be commander-in-chief of the army and navy of the United States. In this respect his authority would be **nominally**[8] the same with that of the king of Great Britain, but in substance much inferior to it. It would amount to nothing more than the supreme command and direction of the military and naval forces, as first General and admiral of the Confederacy; while that of the British king extends to the DECLARING of war and to the RAISING and REGULATING of fleets and armies, all which, by the Constitution under consideration, would **appertain**[9] to the legislature. The governor of New York, on the other hand, is by the constitution of the State vested only with the command of its militia and navy. But the constitutions of several of the States expressly declare their governors to be commanders-in-chief, as well of the army and navy; and it may well be a question, whether those of New Hampshire and Massachusetts, in particular, do not, in this instance, confer larger powers upon their respective governors, than could be claimed by a President of the United States. Thirdly. The power of the President, in respect to pardons, would extend to all cases, EXCEPT THOSE OF IMPEACHMENT. The governor of New York may pardon in all cases, even in those of impeachment, except for treason and murder. Is not the power of the governor, in this article, on a calculation of political consequences, greater than that of the President? All conspiracies and plots against the government, which have not been matured into actual treason, may be screened from punishment of every kind, by the interposition of the prerogative of pardoning. If a governor of New York, therefore, should be at the head of any

---

[8] **nominally**—in name only.

[9] **appertain**—apply.

such conspiracy, until the design had been ripened into actual hostility he could insure his accomplices and adherents an entire **impunity**.[10] A President of the Union, on the other hand, though he may even pardon treason, when prosecuted in the ordinary course of law, could shelter no offender, in any degree, from the effects of impeachment and conviction. Would not the prospect of a total indemnity[11] for all the preliminary steps be a greater temptation to undertake and persevere in an enterprise against the public liberty, than the mere prospect of an exemption from death and confiscation, if the final execution of the design, upon an actual appeal to arms, should miscarry? Would this last expectation have any influence at all, when the probability was computed, that the person who was to afford that exemption might himself be involved in the consequences of the measure, and might be **incapacitated**[12] by his agency in it from affording the desired impunity? The better to judge of this matter, it will be necessary to recollect, that, by the proposed Constitution, the offense of treason is limited "to levying war upon the United States, and adhering to their enemies, giving them aid and comfort"; and that by the laws of New York it is confined within similar bounds. Fourthly. The President can only adjourn the national legislature in the single case of disagreement about the time of adjournment. The British monarch may **prorogue**[13] or even dissolve the Parliament. The governor of New York may also prorogue the legislature of this State for a limited time; a power which, in certain situations, may be employed to very important purposes.

The President is to have power, with the advice and consent of the Senate, to make treaties, provided two

---

[10] **impunity**—exemption from penalty.
[11] **total indemnity**—complete protection.
[12] **incapacitated**—made unable to act.
[13] **prorogue**—postpone.

thirds of the senators present concur. The king of Great Britain is the sole and absolute representative of the nation in all foreign transactions. He can of his own accord make treaties of peace, commerce, alliance, and of every other description. It has been **insinuated**,[14] that his authority in this respect is not conclusive, and that his conventions with foreign powers are subject to the revision, and stand in need of the ratification, of Parliament. But I believe this doctrine was never heard of, until it was broached upon the present occasion. Every **jurist**[15] of that kingdom, and every other man acquainted with its Constitution, knows, as an established fact, that the prerogative of making treaties exists in the crown in its utmost **plenitude**;[16] and that the compacts entered into by the royal authority have the most complete legal validity and perfection, independent of any other sanction. The Parliament, it is true, is sometimes seen employing itself in altering the existing laws to conform them to the stipulations in a new treaty; and this may have possibly given birth to the imagination, that its co-operation was necessary to the obligatory **efficacy**[17] of the treaty. But this parliamentary interposition proceeds from a different cause: from the necessity of adjusting a most artificial and intricate system of revenue and commercial laws to the changes made in them by the operation of the treaty; and of adapting new provisions and precautions to the new state of things, to keep the machine from running into disorder. In this respect, therefore, there is no comparison between the intended power of the President and the actual power of the British sovereign. The one can perform alone what the other can do only with the concurrence of a branch of the legislature. It must be admitted that, in this

---

[14] **insinuated**—implied.
[15] **jurist**—legal scholar.
[16] **plenitude**—abundance; fullness.
[17] **efficacy**—effectiveness.

instance, the power of the federal Executive would exceed that of any State Executive. But this arises naturally from the sovereign power which relates to treaties. If the Confederacy were to be dissolved, it would become a question, whether the Executives of the several States were not solely invested with that delicate and important prerogative.

The President is also to be authorized to receive ambassadors and other public ministers. This, though it has been a rich theme of **declamation**,[18] is more a matter of dignity than of authority. It is a circumstance which will be without consequence in the administration of the government; and it was far more convenient that it should be arranged in this manner, than that there should be a necessity of convening the legislature, or one of its branches, upon every arrival of a foreign minister, though it were merely to take the place of a departed predecessor.

The President is to nominate, and, WITH THE ADVICE AND CONSENT OF THE SENATE, to appoint ambassadors and other public ministers, judges of the Supreme Court, and in general all officers of the United States established by law, and whose appointments are not otherwise provided for by the Constitution. The king of Great Britain is emphatically and truly styled the fountain of honor. He not only appoints to all offices, but can create offices. He can confer titles of nobility at pleasure; and has the disposal of an immense number of church preferments.[19] There is evidently a great inferiority in the power of the President, in this particular, to that of the British king; nor is it equal to that of the governor of New York, if we are to interpret the meaning of the constitution of the State by the practice which has obtained under it. The

---

[18] **declamation**—public debate.
[19] church preferments—promotions of church officials.

power of appointment is with us lodged in a council, composed of the governor and four members of the Senate, chosen by the Assembly. The governor CLAIMS, and has frequently EXERCISED, the right of nomination, and is ENTITLED to a casting vote in the appointment. If he really has the right of nominating, his authority is in this respect equal to that of the President, and exceeds it in the article of the casting vote. In the national government, if the Senate should be divided, no appointment could be made; in the government of New York, if the council should be divided, the governor can turn the scale, and confirm his own nomination. If we compare the publicity which must necessarily attend the mode of appointment by the President and an entire branch of the national legislature, with the privacy in the mode of appointment by the governor of New York, closeted in a secret apartment with at most four, and frequently with only two persons; and if we at the same time consider how much more easy it must be to influence the small number of which a council of appointment consists, than the considerable number of which the national Senate would consist, we cannot hesitate to pronounce that the power of the chief magistrate of this State, in the disposition of offices, must, in practice, be greatly superior to that of the Chief Magistrate of the Union.

Hence it appears that, except as to the concurrent authority of the President in the article of treaties, it would be difficult to determine whether that magistrate would, **in the aggregate**,[20] possess more or less power than the Governor of New York. And it appears yet more unequivocally, that there is no pretense for the parallel which has been attempted between him and the king of Great Britain. But to render the contrast in this

---

[20] **in the aggregate**—on the whole.

respect still more striking, it may be of use to throw the principal circumstances of dissimilitude into a closer group.

The President of the United States would be an officer elected by the people for FOUR years; the king of Great Britain is a perpetual and HEREDITARY prince. The one would be amenable to personal punishment and disgrace; the person of the other is sacred and inviolable. The one would have a QUALIFIED negative upon the acts of the legislative body; the other has an ABSOLUTE negative. The one would have a right to command the military and naval forces of the nation; the other, in addition to this right, possesses that of DECLARING war, and of RAISING and REGULATING fleets and armies by his own authority. The one would have a concurrent power with a branch of the legislature in the formation of treaties; the other is the SOLE POSSESSOR of the power of making treaties. The one would have a like concurrent authority in appointing to offices; the other is the sole author of all appointments. The one can confer no privileges whatever; the other can make **denizens**[21] of aliens, noblemen of commoners; can erect corporations with all the rights incident to corporate bodies. The one can prescribe no rules concerning the commerce or currency of the nation; the other is in several respects the **arbiter**[22] of commerce, and in this capacity can establish markets and fairs, can regulate weights and measures, can lay embargoes for a limited time, can coin money, can authorize or prohibit the circulation of foreign coin. The one has no particle of spiritual jurisdiction; the other is the supreme head and governor of the national church! What answer shall we give to those who would

---

[21] **denizens**—citizens.

[22] **arbiter**—referee.

persuade us that things so unlike resemble each other? The same that ought to be given to those who tell us that a government, the whole power of which would be in the hands of the elective and periodical servants of the people, is an aristocracy, a monarchy, and a despotism.

Publius

QUESTIONS TO CONSIDER

1. According to Hamilton, what important differences exist between the President of the United States and the King of England?

2. What legislative checks on the executive branch does Hamilton cite that support his argument?

3. What differences and similarities exist between the powers of the President and those of the governor of New York?

4. What important criticisms of the Constitution is Hamilton addressing in this *Federalist* paper?

Jackson's Bank Veto

BY PRESIDENT ANDREW JACKSON

Andrew Jackson, a Democrat, was President from 1829 to 1837. He strongly believed that a powerful central government threatened the basic rights and freedoms of ordinary citizens. Earlier, the first Secretary of the Treasury, Alexander Hamilton, had created the Bank of the United States as part of a plan to provide economic stability. Jackson was strongly opposed to the Bank. He felt it established a banking monopoly, limited sources of credit for ordinary citizens, and enriched its stockholders unfairly. In 1832, he used the President's veto power to end it. Ironically, Jackson's use of the veto contributed to a stronger central government. He vetoed twelve bills from Congress during his time in office—in contrast to only nine by all the previous Presidents. His justification was that the President was the only person in government who had been elected by the entire country. His belief that the President, not Congress, should define the national interest dramatically changed the nature of the presidency.

The bill "to modify and continue" the act entitled "An act to incorporate the subscribers to the Bank of the United States" was presented to me on the 4th July instant. Having considered it with that solemn regard to the principles of the Constitution which the day was calculated to inspire, and come to the conclusion that it ought not to become a law, I herewith return it to the Senate, in which it originated, with my objections. A bank of the United States is in many respects convenient for the government and useful to the people. Entertaining this opinion, and deeply impressed with the belief that some of the powers and privileges possessed by the existing bank are unauthorized by the Constitution, **subversive**[1] of the rights of the states, and dangerous to the liberties of the people, I felt it my duty at an early period of my administration to call the attention of Congress to the practicability of organizing an institution combining all its advantages and **obviating**[2] these objections. I sincerely regret that in the act before me I can perceive none of those modifications of the bank charter which are necessary, in my opinion, to make it compatible with justice, with sound policy, or with the Constitution of our country.

The present corporate body, **denominated**[3] the president, directors, and company of the Bank of the United States, will have existed at the time this act is intended to take effect twenty years. It enjoys an exclusive privilege of banking under the authority of the general government, a monopoly of its favor and support, and, as a necessary consequence, almost a monopoly of the foreign and domestic exchange. The powers, privileges, and favors bestowed upon it in the original charter, by increasing the value of the stock far above its par value, operated as a **gratuity**[4] of many millions to the stockholders.[5]

---

[1] **subversive**—undermining.

[2] **obviating**—eliminating.

[3] **denominated**—designated.

[4] **gratuity**—gift.

[5] The bank was funded by both the federal government and wealthy private investors.

An apology may be found for the failure to guard against this result in the consideration that the effect of the original act of incorporation could not be certainly foreseen at the time of its passage. The act before me proposes another gratuity to the holders of the same stock, and in many cases to the same men, of at least $7 million more. This donation finds no apology in any uncertainty as to the effect of the act. On all hands it is conceded that its passage will increase at least 20 or 30 percent more the market price of the stock, subject to the payment of the **annuity**[6] of $200,000 per year secured by the act, thus adding in a moment one-fourth to its par value. It is not our own citizens only who are to receive the bounty of our government. More than $8 million of the stock of this bank are held by foreigners. By this act the American republic proposes virtually to make them a present of some millions of dollars. For these gratuities to foreigners and to some of our own **opulent**[7] citizens the act secures no equivalent whatever. They are the certain gains of the present stockholders under the operation of this act, after making full allowance for the payment of the bonus.

Every monopoly and all exclusive privileges are granted at the expense of the public, which ought to receive a fair equivalent. The many millions which this act proposes to bestow on the stockholders of the existing bank must come directly or indirectly out of the earnings of the American people. It is due to them, therefore, if their government sells monopolies and exclusive privileges, that they should at least exact for them as much as they are worth in open market. The value of the monopoly in this case may be correctly **ascertained**.[8] The $28 million of stock would probably be at an advance of 50 percent and command in market at

---

[6] **annuity**—annual yield.

[7] **opulent**—wealthy.

[8] **ascertained**—determined.

least $42 million, subject to the payment of the present bonus. The present value of the monopoly, therefore, is $17 million, and this the act proposes to sell for $3 million, payable in fifteen annual installments of $200,000 each . . . .

It is maintained by the advocates of the bank that its constitutionality in all its features ought to be considered as settled by **precedent**[9] and by the decision of the Supreme Court. To this conclusion I cannot assent. Mere precedent is a dangerous source of authority and should not be regarded as deciding questions of constitutional power except where the **acquiescence**[10] of the people and the states can be considered as well settled. So far from this being the case on this subject, an argument against the bank might be based on precedent. One Congress in 1791 decided in favor of a bank; another in 1811 decided against it. One Congress in 1815 decided against a bank; another in 1816 decided in its favor. Prior to the present Congress, therefore, the precedents drawn from that source were equal. If we resort to the states, the expressions of legislative, judicial, and executive opinions against the bank have been probably to those in its favor as four to one. There is nothing in precedent, therefore, which, if its authority were admitted, ought to weigh in favor of the act before me.

If the opinion of the Supreme Court covered the whole ground of this act, it ought not to control the coordinate authorities of this government. The Congress, the executive, and the court must each for itself be guided by its own opinion of the Constitution. Each public officer who takes an oath to support the Constitution swears that he will support it as he understands it and not as it is understood by others. It is as much the duty of the House of Representatives, of

---

[9] **precedent**—pattern or rule for future similar actions.
[10] **acquiescence**—approval.

the Senate, and of the President to decide upon the constitutionality of any bill or resolution which may be presented to them for passage or approval as it is of the supreme judges when it may be brought before them for judicial decision. The opinion of the judges has no more authority over Congress than the opinion of Congress has over the judges, and on that point the President is independent of both. The authority of the Supreme Court must not, therefore, be permitted to control the Congress or the executive when acting in their legislative capacities, but to have only such influence as the force of their reasoning may deserve. . . .

It is to be regretted that the rich and powerful too often bend the acts of government to their selfish purposes. Distinctions in society will always exist under every just government. Equality of talents, of education, or of wealth cannot be produced by human institutions. In the full enjoyment of the gifts of Heaven and the fruits of superior industry, economy, and virtue, every man is equally entitled to protection by law; but when the laws undertake to add to these natural and just advantages artificial distinctions, to grant titles, gratuities, and exclusive privileges, to make the rich richer and the potent more powerful, the humble members of society—the farmers, mechanics, and laborers—who have neither the time nor the means of securing like favors to themselves, have a right to complain of the injustice of their government. There are no necessary evils in government. Its evils exist only in its abuses. If it would confine itself to equal protection, and, as Heaven does its rains, shower its favors alike on the high and the low, the rich and the poor, it would be an unqualified blessing. In the act before me there seems to be a wide and unnecessary departure from these just principles.

Nor is our government to be maintained or our Union preserved by invasions of the rights and powers of the several states. In thus attempting to make our general government strong, we make it weak. Its true strength consists in leaving individuals and states as much as possible to themselves—in making itself felt, not in its power, but in its **beneficence**;[11] not in its control, but in its protection; not in binding the states more closely to the center, but leaving each to move unobstructed in its proper orbit.

Experience should teach us wisdom. Most of the difficulties our government now encounters and most of the dangers which **impend**[12] over our Union have sprung from an abandonment of the legitimate objects of government by our national legislation and the adoption of such principles as are embodied in this act. Many of our rich men have not been content with equal protection and equal benefits but have besought us to make them richer by act of Congress. By attempting to gratify their desires, we have in the results of our legislation arrayed section against section, interest against interest, and man against man, in a fearful commotion which threatens to shake the foundations of our Union.

It is time to pause in our career to review our principles and, if possible, revive that devoted patriotism and spirit of compromise which distinguished the **sages**[13] of the Revolution and the fathers of our Union. If we cannot at once, in justice to interests vested under **improvident**[14] legislation, make our government what it ought to be, we can at least take a stand against all new

---

[11] **beneficence**—kind, generous acts.

[12] **impend**—hang.

[13] **sages**—very wise people.

[14] **improvident**—unwise; failing to provide for future needs.

grants of monopolies and exclusive privileges, against any prostitution of our government to the advancement of a few at the expense of the many, and in favor of compromise and gradual reform in our code of laws and system of political economy.

QUESTIONS TO CONSIDER

1. What are Jackson's primary reasons for vetoing the bank bill?

2. What are Jackson's criticisms of the legislative and judicial branches in regard to their treatment of the bank?

3. What beliefs about democracy does Jackson's veto reflect?

4. How did Jackson's frequent use of the veto increase the power of the presidency?

5. Does Jackson's use of the veto contradict his beliefs about democracy? Why or why not?

Against Packing the Supreme Court

BY DOROTHY THOMPSON

The balance of power among branches of government usually tilts toward the executive during times of crisis. The Great Depression was one of those times. President Franklin Roosevelt (1933 to 1945) concentrated policy-making power in his office with help from his "Brain Trust" advisers. Roosevelt's Democratic Party controlled Congress by huge majorities, and until 1937 it passed virtually every law that Roosevelt wanted. However, the Supreme Court, which was largely made up of conservative justices appointed by past Republican Presidents, was not so cooperative. In 1937, when the Court declared one of Roosevelt's most valued agencies unconstitutional, the President proposed to add justices to the Court. He asked Congress to increase the seats on the Court from nine to fifteen to offset those justices aged 70 or more. Critics accused Roosevelt of trying to pack the Court with his own supporters. This excerpt, by the respected Washington Star columnist Dorothy Thompson, provides the arguments that helped Congress defeat Roosevelt's proposal.

If the American people accept this last **audacity**[1] of the President without letting out a yell to high heaven, they have ceased to be jealous of their liberties and are ripe for ruin.

This is the beginning of pure personal government. Do you want it? Do you like it? Look around about the world—there are plenty of examples [e.g., Hitler[2]]—and make up your mind.

The Executive is already powerful by reason of his overwhelming [re-election] victory in November, and will be strengthened even more if the reorganization plan for the administration, presented some weeks ago, is adopted. We have, to all intents and purposes, a one-party Congress, dominated by the President. Although nearly 40 percent of the voters **repudiated**[3] the New Deal at the polls, they have less than 20 percent representation in both houses of Congress. And now the Supreme Court is to have a majority determined by the President and by a Senate which he dominates.

When that happens we will have a one-man Government. It will all be constitutional. So, he claims, is Herr Hitler.

Leave the personality and the intentions of the President out of the picture. They are not the crux of this issue. He may be as wise as Solon,[4] lofty as Plato,[5] and pure as Parsifal.[6] He may have the liberties of the American people deeply at heart. But he will have a successor who may be none of these things. There have been benevolent dictatorships and benevolent tyrannies.

---

[1] **audacity**—shameless boldness; impudence.

[2] Adolf Hitler—Germany's chancellor from 1933 to 1945. At the time this article was written, Hitler had assumed dictatorial powers and was building up the German military to invade other European countries.

[3] **repudiated**—rejected.

[4] Solon—a lawgiver in ancient Athens.

[5] Plato—a famous Athenian philosopher.

[6] Parsifal—in legend, a faithful knight of King Arthur's Round Table who searched for the Holy Grail.

They have even, at times in history, worked for the popular welfare. But that is not the welfare which, up to now, the American people have chosen.

And let us not be confused by the words "liberal" and "conservative" or misled into thinking that the expressed will of the majority is the essence of democracy. By that definition Hitler, Stalin, and Mussolini are all great democratic leaders. The essence of democracy is the protection of minorities.

Nor has a majority of this generation the right to **mortgage**[7] a majority of the next. In the Constitution of the United States are incorporated the rights of the people, rights enjoyed by every American citizen **in perpetuity**,[8] which cannot be voted away by any majority, ever.

Majorities are temporary things. The Supreme Court is there to protect the fundamental law even against the momentary "will of the people." That is its function. And it is precisely because nine men can walk out and say: "You can't do that!" that our liberties are protected against the mob urge that occasionally overcomes democracies. That is why the Supreme Court has been traditionally divorced from momentary majorities. . . .

The Constitution can be changed. There are ways provided for doing so. To change it will require much deliberation, debate, time. And what is wrong with deliberation and debate and time? What is the hurry? Under what threat are we living at this instant?

This is no proposal to change the Constitution. This is no proposal to limit the powers of the Supreme Court. This is a proposal to capture the Supreme Court . . .

If, of the six men over 70, four had been "liberals" and two "conservatives," instead of the other way around, do you think that this program would have been proposed? . . .

---

[7] **mortgage**—burden; put at risk.
[8] **in perpetuity**—forever.

Don't talk of liberalism! The liberal does not believe that the end justifies the means. Long experience has taught him that the means usually determine the end. No human being can believe in the sincerity of this proposal. It is clever, in a world sick of cleverness and longing for plain talk and simple honesty. Must we begin to examine every message from the President to see whether there is a trick in it somewhere?

QUESTIONS TO CONSIDER

1. What did Thompson mean when she wrote that Roosevelt's action "is the beginning of pure personal government"?

2. According to Thompson, in what ways does the Supreme Court protect the rights of the minority? How would Roosevelt's action undermine this protection?

3. What did "liberalism" and "conservatism" have to do with Roosevelt's proposed program?

4. In what way is Roosevelt's proposal a "trick"?

from

Shadow

BY BOB WOODWARD

*So much power was in the President's hands that by the early
1970s Republican Richard Nixon's term was criticized as the
"imperial presidency." The balance of power changed, however, with
the Watergate crisis of 1973–74. Nixon and his advisers were
accused of covering up a break-in at the Democratic Party headquarters in the Watergate building during the 1972 election
campaign. Congress sponsored investigations into alleged illegal
acts and abuses of power by the Nixon White House. Ultimately,
the House Judiciary Committee recommended impeachment, and
the Supreme Court forced the President to release secret tape
recordings. These proved he knew about the cover-up. In August
1974, Nixon gave up his fight to remain in office and resigned—
something no President had done before. Then Vice President
Gerald Ford had to decide whether to pardon Nixon or allow him
to be indicted on criminal charges. When he chose to pardon
Nixon it set off an enormous controversy. Bob Woodward of* The
Washington Post *shared a Pulitzer Prize for helping uncover the
scandal. His 1999 book* Shadow *focused on how Watergate
impacted future presidencies.*

August 1, 1974, was a hot Washington summer morning with the humidity heavy in the air, but inside Richard Nixon's air-conditioned White House it was unnaturally cool. The President looked thin, battered, at times almost like a stroke victim. His chief of staff Alexander M. Haig Jr.'s eyes were red. Early that morning Nixon had summoned Haig, a 49-year-old Army general who had been his right-hand man for the previous 15 months, the most grueling, emotionally exhausting and politically unstable of the Watergate scandal. The **incessant**[1] hangover of sleep deprivation had become a way of life for both.

"Al, it's over," Nixon said in a surprisingly impersonal, even matter-of-fact tone. Nixon, ever the political realist, said he simply couldn't govern. His presidency was collapsing. He could almost hear the air rushing out of it—power leaving. All three branches of the federal government had turned against the president. Although Special Watergate Prosecutor Leon Jaworski worked for the executive branch that Nixon headed, he was conducting an independent, relentless investigation. A week earlier the Supreme Court, in a unanimous decision, had ruled in the special prosecutor's favor that Nixon had to turn over an additional 64 secret White House tape recordings. Two of those tapes, once released, were going to undermine Nixon and show he ordered the Watergate cover-up. In the legislative branch, a lopsided bipartisan majority of the Judiciary Committee of the House of Representatives had days earlier voted three articles recommending his impeachment based on information that Special Prosecutor Jaworski had provided through the grand jury to the House committee. Governing had been reduced to a series of stopgap pretenses.

---

[1] **incessant**—unending.

Typically Nixon had a plan. He intended to announce his resignation in four days, he told Haig. He needed the weekend to take his family to Camp David, the presidential retreat in the nearby Maryland mountains, and prepare them. He expected his wife and two grown daughters, Julie and Tricia, to resist and fight his decision with every bone in their bodies.

"It might be better to resign tomorrow night and leave town immediately," Haig proposed.

"No," Nixon answered. Nixon's tone was at first gentle. Then he shifted and became gruff, waving a forefinger at Haig as he so often had, demanding his orders be followed. "This is my decision and mine alone," Nixon insisted, warning that he would not succumb to political pressure from Republicans, the Congress or his cabinet. "I've resisted political pressure all my life, and if I get it now, I may change my mind."

"Understood, Mr. President," Haig answered.

Nixon directed Haig to inform Vice President Gerald Ford that he should be ready to assume the presidency, but not to give him all the facts. "Tell him I want absolute secrecy. Tell him what's coming. Explain the reasoning. But don't tell him when."

Watergate had put the presidency in play. The President's hold on the office was loosened as Nixon contemplated resigning. It was a singular moment in American history, creating a dangerous new space in which Nixon, Ford and Haig had to operate. Where exactly was presidential power at that moment? Nixon held the office, according to the law and Constitution. Ford was stumbling to the presidency. For his part, Haig, mindful of his multiple and competing loyalties to Nixon, Ford and the country, was to be the **broker**[2] and go-between.

---

[2] **broker**—negotiator.

There was no steady hand. Nixon was consumed by a simmering, explosive anger that he was getting a bum rap. He was emotionally disabled, depressed and **paranoid**.[3] Ford had acquired none of the armor that comes with brutal presidential or vice presidential campaigning. He had no real executive experience. He had never run for a national office, having been appointed vice president by Nixon—and confirmed by Congress under the 25th Amendment—to replace Spiro Agnew, who had resigned the previous year in a financial scandal. He was a man of the House of Representatives, where from 1948 to 1973 he had represented his Grand Rapids, Michigan, district.

Haig also was somewhat ill-equipped. . . . But as an Army officer he was used to taking orders and getting the job done. He had received his basic bureaucratic education in the school of maneuver and deception run by Henry Kissinger[4] in the National Security Council staff where he had served as deputy.

That same day, Kissinger, now the secretary of state, told Haig, "We've got to quietly bring down the curtain on this charade."

Before he saw Ford, Haig met in his West Wing corner office with Nixon's White House Watergate lawyer, J. Fred Buzhardt, a diminutive, soft-spoken Southerner who had previously worked as Pentagon general counsel. Both were West Point graduates. . . . They had become close over the last year. It was a partnership in survival. . . . What was the legal situation if Nixon resigned? Haig asked.

Buzhardt. . . had a set of options to present to the Vice President. All, with one exception, focused on Nixon—not Ford.

---

[3] **paranoid**—unreasonably suspicious.

[4] Henry Kissinger—a prominent statesman of the 1970s. He served as Nixon's foreign policy adviser and secretary of state.

Haig felt it was sensible to concentrate on Nixon. He was still President. They served him, and, as Haig knew, Nixon was an exhaustive explorer of alternatives.

Buzhardt had thought out six possibilities. . . and two of those included [Nixon] granting a pardon to himself. The sixth alternative: Nixon could resign and hope his successor, Ford, would pardon him. This last one was fleshed out more than the others, spelled out in detail.

"Here's what you should give him," Buzhardt said, handing Haig two sheets of yellow legal paper for the meeting with the Vice President.

Ford was on the cusp of assuming the highest office in the land, the leadership of the free world, and Buzhardt was focused on what could be done for Nixon. Haig realized that Buzhardt might be planting a pardon suggestion.

Before 9 a.m., Haig went to Ford's office.

Ford, then 61, had been Vice President only eight months. A warm Midwesterner, whose speech was slow, deliberate—and at times awkward—Ford had been grafted onto the Nixon administration as a necessary afterthought. Under the Constitution, Nixon had to have a Vice President. Nixon **deemed**[5] his preferred choices too controversial, ideological or dynamic to win confirmation, especially former Texas Governor John Connally. "This left Jerry Ford," Nixon wrote in his memoirs. Nixon knew that Ford was loyal, a creature of the Republican party, having served 24 years in the House, nine of those as Republican minority leader. To Nixon, Ford was basically a party chore boy who undertook unsavory tasks. . . . With Nixon bogged down in his Watergate defense, Ford had been almost on his own as Vice President, **peripheral**[6] to the administration.

---

[5] **deemed**—believed; judged.

[6] **peripheral**—nonessential; on the outskirts.

Ford had Robert Hartmann, a top aide and former newspaperman, with him when Haig arrived in the office. Haig detested and distrusted Hartmann. He had received reports from the Secret Service[7] that Hartmann would drink late at night in his office. So Haig told Ford only that a new tape recording about to be released would present grave difficulties for Nixon in an impeachment trial.

Later in the day Haig called the Vice President and asked for a second meeting, this time alone. Ford agreed. At 3:30 p.m. Haig entered the Vice President's suite. He looked troubled and on edge. He had just read the transcripts of two tape recordings made six days after the June 17, 1972, Watergate break-in. Nixon ordered the cover-up. His case would collapse when the tapes were made public. There was a decorated screen in one corner of the room. Haig later said he was certain that Hartmann was stationed behind the screen to take notes in secret and to protect Ford, a charge both Hartmann and Ford categorically deny. But the air was filled with distrust.

"Are you ready, Mr. Vice President, to assume the presidency in a short period of time?"

Ford, absolutely stunned, said he was prepared.

Haig wanted his assessment of the situation, but Ford did not have a lot to say. "These are what the lawyers think," Haig told Ford, taking out the papers Buzhardt had given him.

The options for Nixon and others in the White House were numerous. Nixon could step aside temporarily under the 25th Amendment, he could just wait and delay the impeachment process, or he could try to settle for a formal censure.[8] In addition, there were

---

[7] The Secret Service is a division of the Treasury Department whose job it is to protect the President. In this case, the Secret Service was spying on a top aide of Vice President Ford.

[8] censure—reprimand voted by the Senate.

three pardon options. Nixon could pardon himself and resign. Or he could pardon the aides involved in Watergate and then resign.

Or, Haig said, Nixon could agree to leave in return for an agreement that the new President would pardon him. Haig handed Ford the papers. The first sheet contained a handwritten summary of a President's legal authority to pardon. The second sheet was a draft pardon form that only needed Ford's signature and Nixon's name to make it legal.

Haig asked for Ford's recommendation about what course Nixon might follow. Haig privately believed that this was a time for mercy if ever there were one. A pardon would be an act of simple humanity. It would spare the country a Senate trial[9] that would create a destructive heritage of hatred and resentment. It would be patriotic and courageous, in his eyes.

Even if Haig offered no direct words on his views, the message was almost certainly sent. An emotional man, Haig was incapable of concealing his feelings; those who worked closely with him rarely found him ambiguous[10]. . . . It was part of his style—to convey his attitude, and not just through words.

Ford dwelled on the pardon possibilities.

"It is my understanding from a White House lawyer," Haig said, "that a President does have authority to grant a pardon even before criminal action has been taken against an individual." Of course, Nixon was the only major Watergate player against whom the special prosecutor had not taken criminal action. . . .

---

[9] Under the impeachment process, the House must vote to "impeach" a President or other government official—in other words, to formally charge him with wrongdoing. The Senate then must conduct a trial on these charges and vote on whether to convict the President and remove him from office.

[10] **ambiguous**—indefinite.

Ford summoned Hartmann. He extracted another solemn pledge of secrecy.

Hartmann promised.

Ford said Haig had reported that Nixon was going to resign because of new, damaging tapes. Haig had listed some alternatives for the endgame, among them the possibility that Nixon could agree to leave in return for an agreement that he, Ford, as President, would pardon Nixon.

"Jesus!" Hartmann said aloud. "What did you tell him?"

"I told him I needed time to think about it."

"You what?" Hartmann fairly shouted. Ford's willingness to entertain a discussion of a pardon was probably all Haig and Nixon wanted or needed. Even entertaining any agreement of resignation for a pardon, Hartmann believed, was outrageous. Ford had already committed a monstrous **impropriety**[11] and the damage that had been done was irreversible. Hartmann felt it could taint a Ford presidency forever, linking even a voluntary resignation to discussions of an eventual pardon and perhaps an expectation, at least implied, of a pardon from Ford.

Ford didn't agree. Nothing had been promised. He wanted to talk to his wife, Betty.

Hartmann thought that was a good idea. . . . She could gently turn her husband off Haig more effectively than he could.

Late that night Ford told his wife about Haig's alternatives. She was firm in her view that her husband shouldn't get involved in making any recommendations at all. Not to Haig, not to Nixon, not to anybody. Ford seemed to get the message. . . .

The next morning, Friday, August 2, Haig and Buzhardt discussed at length Ford's late night phone

---

[11] **impropriety**—improper action.

call. They concluded that there was some real trouble brewing around Ford.

Over in the Vice President's suite of offices in the Old Executive Office Building that morning Ford brought in a second aide, Jack Marsh, a former Virginia congressman, for advice on Haig's pardon conversation. . . . Marsh had never seen the Vice President with such a grim expression. Ford looked like he had just been told that his house with all his family in it had burned to the ground, destroying everything and everyone.

"I want you to swear you will not reveal what I'm about to tell you," Ford said to Marsh.

Marsh assented.

Ford explained that the previous day Haig had said explicitly that new tapes were going to force Nixon's resignation. Ford went through the alternatives that Haig had presented, including the one in which Nixon resigned. "I then, what I would do, I would give Nixon a pardon," Ford said.

Marsh couldn't believe it. He tried to remain calm. He could see that Ford hoped he would say, "It's the kind of thing, Jerry, you need to do." But Marsh saw the danger. "Look, you can't do this," he said gently.

Ford was standing. He slowly pulled the two pieces of yellow legal paper out of his pocket and handed them to Marsh. "You could make a strong case for a pardon, that it would be in the national interest," Ford said. He seemed to be advocating Haig's arguments for granting Nixon a pardon.

"You can't do that," Marsh said. It could look like or be a **quid pro quo**[12] for Nixon's resignation.

Ford didn't see it.

Marsh knew that Ford could be stubborn once he made up his mind. He was concerned that without

---

[12] **quid pro quo**—deal. From Latin, it translates as "this for that."

further advice, Ford might just go ahead with a pardon. Of the alternatives listed by Haig, Marsh could see that Ford was concentrating on the one that involved him. He was going to become president, and perhaps the best and smoothest way was to grant a pardon. Marsh said he had no problem with Ford considering a pardon but not while he was vice president. As the constitutional successor, he couldn't consider a pardon. He knew the law. It was illegal to offer anything of value—as a pardon surely would be—in exchange for a federal office. It shouldn't even be discussed, much less considered.

Marsh and Hartmann talked again to Ford.

Ford was now emotional, saying he had told Haig that Watergate had to stop, that it was tearing the country to pieces. With some contradiction, Ford said he had decided to go ahead and get it over with, so he had called Haig the previous night and told him they should do whatever they decided to do. It was all right with Ford, but there was no agreement.

Hartmann and Marsh were stunned. This version of Ford's call to Haig was significantly more alarming than what they had earlier heard. Both men tried to **elicit**[13] what exact words had passed between Ford and Haig, but they couldn't get clear statements. Ford obviously just wanted the matter closed. . . .

Hartmann and Marsh left the Vice President disturbed.

"We got to stop him," Marsh said. "We got to stop him cold right now."

Hartmann was worried that Ford had already decided to grant a pardon. They drew up a list of ten people that Ford might consult. Who might agree with them and be able to persuade Ford? They put Betty Ford

---

[13] **elicit**—bring to light.

at the top of the list, but they felt it would not be appropriate to enlist her. Second on the list was Bryce Harlow, a former Nixon White House counselor and one of the wise old men of Republican politics.

At their request, Ford agreed to see Harlow. Hartmann and Marsh poured out their fears to Harlow before he met with Ford. A small, charming, passionate but wordy man, Harlow listened to them and agreed. It was a disaster. The three went to see the Vice President.

Haig was carrying out a mission for Nixon, Harlow said, and Ford was in grave danger of compromising his presidency and independence. He said the Vice President had to protect himself and ensure that no one could cry deal if Ford later granted Nixon a pardon. "But the most urgent thing, Mr. Vice President," Harlow said, "is to tell Al Haig, straight out and unequivocally, that whatever discussions you and he had yesterday and last night were purely hypothetical and conversational, that you will in no manner, affirmatively or negatively, advise him or the President as to his future course, and nothing you may have said is to be represented to the President, or to anyone else, to the contrary."

It was a lawyer's mouthful. But Ford realized the three men were right. He had been **naive**.[14] He agreed to call Haig to make it clear that he had never accepted the proffered deal. Harlow wrote out what he should say.

Ford called Haig and told him he had no intention of recommending what President Nixon should do about resigning or not resigning. Nothing they had talked about the previous afternoon should be given any consideration in whatever decision the President might make. . . .

---

[14] **naive**—innocent; uninformed.

Ford decided both he and Haig would be better off if they never again sat down and talked about the options. The heart of the matter, Ford believed, was that one way or the other Nixon was going to go. Ford's first concern was that he was about to become President—a job he had never sought. Now it was dropping in his lap. His second major worry was that he really didn't want to become President.

By that evening of August 2, 1974, Haig had a bigger problem. Nixon called to say he had changed his mind about resignation.

"Let them impeach me," Nixon told his chief of staff. "We'll fight it out to the end."

The next day, August 3, the Vice President was traveling. In Hattiesburg, Mississippi, he held a press conference. The reporters were interested in Watergate. One noted that Ford's press secretary had mentioned that Ford had met with Haig two days earlier to discuss impeachment. What was going on and what was Ford's attitude?

"I have met with Al Haig," Ford said. "I don't think this is unusual." Rather than evade the question, the Vice President lied. The purpose of the meeting, he said, was to discuss "what could be done, if anything, to convince the members of the House that the President was innocent as both of us feel.". . .

Later that day in New Orleans, asked again about the meeting with Haig, Ford once more deceived. "It was not an extraordinary meeting," he said, "if that's what you want me to say. It was an ordinary meeting of the kind that we frequently have and has no extraordinary implications."

Ford's statement was, of course, the opposite of what had occurred. It was more than extraordinary. The presidency would probably never be the same.

Amid the uncertainty, distrust and secrecy of their small meetings, Nixon, Haig, Ford and three Ford advisers were reshaping the presidency, making the first decisions of a new era. Perhaps for the first time the presidency was to be considered a resignable office.

QUESTIONS TO CONSIDER

1. What roles did the legislative and judicial branches play in bringing about Nixon's resignation?

2. Did presidential advisers, such as Alexander Haig and Robert Hartmann, have too much power in shaping President Ford's decision to grant Nixon a pardon? Why or why not?

3. Did President Ford make a mistake when he granted Nixon a pardon? Why or why not?

4. Woodward argues that the "shadow" of Watergate made the presidency a "resignable" office. Do you agree? Explain your answer.

The Impeachment
of Bill Clinton

BY REPUBLICAN MEMBERS OF THE HOUSE
JUDICIARY COMMITTEE

The impeachment process is designed to provide the legislative
branch of government, Congress, with an important safeguard against
illegal actions by anyone holding high government office, including
the President. Twenty-four years after Republican Richard Nixon
resigned to avoid being impeached, the impeachment process was
brought against another President, Democrat Bill Clinton. Elected in
1992 and re-elected in 1996, Clinton often was at odds with the
Republican-controlled Congress. In 1998, Clinton was accused of
lying under oath and abusing his office in attempting to cover up a
sexual relationship with a young White House intern, Monica
Lewinsky. The Judiciary Committee of the House of Representatives
brought four draft articles of impeachment before the full House,
and Clinton was impeached on Articles I and III. In the Senate
trial, Clinton was acquitted by a vote of 55 to 45 on Article I, and
by a vote of 50 to 50 on Article III. Clinton remained in office.

Text of the draft articles of impeachment offered by Republican members of the House Judiciary Committee:
Resolved, That William Jefferson Clinton, President of the United States, is impeached for high crimes and misdemeanors, and that the following articles of impeachment be exhibited to the United States Senate:

Articles of impeachment exhibited by the House of Representatives of the United States of America in the name of itself and of the people of the United States of America, against William Jefferson Clinton, President of the United States of America, in maintenance and support of its impeachment against him for high crimes and misdemeanors.

Article I
In his conduct while President of the United States, William Jefferson Clinton, in violation of his constitutional oath faithfully to execute the office of President of the United States and, to the best of his ability, preserve, protect, and defend the Constitution of the United States, and in violation of his constitutional duty to take care that the laws be faithfully executed, has willfully corrupted and manipulated the judicial process of the United States for his personal gain and **exoneration,**[1] impeding the administration of justice, in that:

On August 17, 1998, William Jefferson Clinton swore to tell the truth, the whole truth, and nothing but the truth before a Federal grand jury of the United States. Contrary to that oath, William Jefferson Clinton willfully provided perjurious, false and misleading testimony to the grand jury[2] concerning: (1) the nature

---

[1] **exoneration**—the finding of innocence; acquittal.

[2] Clinton's presidency was marred by numerous charges of illegal activities alleged to have taken place earlier, when he was governor of Arkansas. Under pressure from Congress, Attorney General Janet Reno appointed a special prosecutor to investigate. He, in turn, convened a grand jury to hear evidence.

and details of his relationship with a subordinate government employee;[3] (2) prior perjurious, false and misleading testimony he gave in a Federal civil rights action[4] brought against him; (3) prior false and misleading statements he allowed his attorney to make to a Federal judge in that civil rights action; and (4) his corrupt efforts to influence the testimony of witnesses[5] and to impede the discovery of evidence in that civil rights action.

In doing this, William Jefferson Clinton has undermined the integrity of his office, has brought disrepute on the Presidency, has betrayed his trust as President, and has acted in a manner subversive of the rule of law and justice, to the manifest injury of the people of the United States.

Wherefore, William Jefferson Clinton, by such conduct, warrants impeachment and trial, and removal from office and disqualification to hold and enjoy any office of honor, trust or profit under the United States.

Article II

In his conduct while President of the United States, William Jefferson Clinton, in violation of his constitutional oath faithfully to execute the office of President of the United States and, to the best of his ability, preserve, protect, and defend the Constitution of the United States, and in violation of his constitutional duty to take care that the laws be faithfully executed, has willfully corrupted and manipulated the judicial process of the United States for his personal gain and exoneration, impeding the administration of justice, in that:

---

[3] subordinate government employee—Monica Lewinsky.

[4] Federal civil rights action—a sexual harassment suit brought by a former state of Arkansas employee, Paula Jones.

[5] Jones's lawyers had required Monica Lewinsky to testify about her alleged relationship with Bill Clinton. The charge is that Clinton tried to get her, and others, to make false statements.

(1) On December 23, 1997, William Jefferson Clinton, in sworn answers to written questions asked as part of a Federal civil rights action brought against him, willfully provided perjurious, false and misleading testimony in response to questions deemed relevant by a Federal judge concerning conduct and proposed conduct with subordinate employees.

(2) On January 17, 1998, William Jefferson Clinton swore under oath to tell the truth, the whole truth, and nothing but the truth in a **deposition**[6] given as part of a Federal civil rights action brought against him. Contrary to that oath, William Jefferson Clinton willfully provided perjurious, false and misleading testimony in response to questions deemed relevant by a Federal judge concerning the nature and details of his relationship with a subordinate government employee and his corrupt efforts to influence the testimony of that employee.

In all of this, William Jefferson Clinton has undermined the integrity of his office, has brought disrepute on the Presidency, has betrayed his trust as President, and has acted in a manner subversive of the rule of law and justice, to the manifest injury of the people of the United States.

Wherefore, William Jefferson Clinton, by such conduct, warrants impeachment and trial, and removal from office and disqualification to hold and enjoy any office of honor, trust or profit under the United States.

Article III
In his conduct while President of the United States, William Jefferson Clinton, in violation of his constitutional oath faithfully to execute the office of President of

---

[6] **deposition**—testimony given by a witness, usually taken before a trial begins.

the United States and, to the best of his ability, preserve, protect, and defend the Constitution of the United States, and in violation of his constitutional duty to take care that the laws be faithfully executed, has prevented, obstructed, and impeded the administration of justice, and has to that end engaged personally, and through his subordinates and agents, in a course of conduct or scheme designed to delay, impede, cover up, and conceal the existence of evidence and testimony related to a Federal civil rights action brought against him in a duly instituted judicial proceeding.

The means used to implement this course of conduct or scheme included one or more of the following acts:

(1) On or about December 17, 1997, William Jefferson Clinton corruptly encouraged a witness in a Federal civil rights action brought against him to execute a sworn affidavit in that proceeding that he knew to be perjurious, false and misleading.

(2) On or about December 17, 1997, William Jefferson Clinton corruptly encouraged a witness in a Federal civil rights action brought against him to give perjurious, false and misleading testimony if and when called to testify personally in that proceeding.

(3) On or about December 28, 1997, William Jefferson Clinton corruptly engaged in, encouraged, or supported a scheme to conceal evidence that had been subpoenaed in a Federal civil rights action brought against him.

(4) Beginning on or about December 7, 1997, and continuing through and including January 14, 1998, William Jefferson Clinton intensified and succeeded in an effort to secure job assistance to a witness[7] in a Federal civil rights action brought against him in order

---

[7] witness—Monica Lewinsky.

to corruptly prevent the truthful testimony of that witness in that proceeding at a time when the truthful testimony of that witness would have been harmful to him.

(5) On January 17, 1998, at his deposition in a Federal civil rights action brought against him, William Jefferson Clinton corruptly allowed his attorney to make false and misleading statements to a Federal judge characterizing an affidavit, in order to prevent questioning deemed relevant by the judge. Such false and misleading statements were subsequently acknowledged by his attorney in a communication to that judge.

(6) On or about January 18 and January 20–21, 1998, William Jefferson Clinton related a false and misleading account of events relevant to a Federal civil rights action brought against him to a potential witness in that proceeding, in order to corruptly influence the testimony of that witness.

(7) On or about January 21, 23 and 26, 1998, William Jefferson Clinton made false and misleading statements to potential witnesses[8] in a Federal grand jury proceeding in order to corruptly influence the testimony of those witnesses. The false and misleading statements made by William Jefferson Clinton were repeated by the witnesses to the grand jury, causing the grand jury to receive false and misleading information.

In all of this, William Jefferson Clinton has undermined the integrity of his office, has brought disrepute on the Presidency, has betrayed his trust as President, and has acted in a manner subversive of the rule of law and justice, to the manifest injury of the people of the United States.

---

[8] potential witnesses—aides, advisers, White House employees; anyone that might have observed or heard about the alleged Clinton/Lewinsky relationship.

Wherefore, William Jefferson Clinton, by such conduct, warrants impeachment and trial, and removal from office and disqualification to hold and enjoy any office of honor, trust or profit under the United States.

Article IV

Using the powers and influence of the office of President of the United States, William Jefferson Clinton, in violation of his constitutional oath faithfully to execute the office of President of the United States and, to the best of his ability, preserve, protect, and defend the Constitution of the United States, and in disregard of his constitutional duty to take care that the laws be faithfully executed, has repeatedly engaged in conduct that resulted in misuse and abuse of his high office, impaired the due and proper administration of justice and the conduct of lawful inquiries, and contravened the laws governing the integrity of the judicial and legislative branches and the truth-seeking purpose of coordinate investigative proceedings.

This misuse and abuse of office has included one or more of the following:

(1) As President, using the attributes of office, William Jefferson Clinton willfully made false and misleading public statements for the purpose of deceiving the people of the United States in order to continue concealing his misconduct and to escape accountability for such misconduct.[9]

(2) As President, using the attributes of office, William Jefferson Clinton willfully made false and misleading statements to members of his cabinet, and White House aides, so that these Federal employees would repeat such false and misleading statements publicly, thereby utilizing public resources for the

---

[9] Clinton later admitted he had, in fact, misled the public.

purpose of deceiving the people of the United States, in order to continue concealing his misconduct and to escape accountability for such misconduct. The false and misleading statements made by William Jefferson Clinton to members of his cabinet and White House aides were repeated by those members and aides, causing the people of the United States to receive false and misleading information from high government officials.

(3) As President, using the Office of White House Counsel, William Jefferson Clinton **frivolously**[10] and corruptly asserted executive privilege,[11] which is intended to protect from disclosure communications regarding the constitutional functions of the Executive, and which may be exercised only by the President, with respect to communications other than those regarding the constitutional functions of the Executive, for the purpose of delaying and obstructing a Federal criminal investigation and the proceedings of a Federal grand jury.

(4) As President, William Jefferson Clinton refused and failed to respond to certain written requests for admission and willfully made perjurious, false and misleading sworn statements in response to certain written requests for admission propounded to him as part of the impeachment inquiry authorized by the House of Representatives of the Congress of the United States. William Jefferson Clinton, in refusing and failing to respond and in making perjurious, false and misleading statements, assumed to himself functions and judgments necessary to the exercise of the sole power of impeachment vested by the Constitution in the House of Representatives and exhibited contempt for the inquiry.

---

[10] **frivolously**—thoughtlessly.
[11] executive privilege—the right of a President to withhold confidential information from the public, usually for reasons of national security.

In all of this, William Jefferson Clinton has undermined the integrity of his office, has brought disrepute on the Presidency, has betrayed his trust as President, and has acted in a manner subversive of the rule of law and justice, to the manifest injury of the people of the United States.

Wherefore, William Jefferson Clinton, by such conduct, warrants impeachment and trial, and removal from office and disqualification to hold and enjoy any office of honor, trust or profit under the United States.

QUESTIONS TO CONSIDER

1. In your opinion, do the charges in the articles of impeachment represent "high crimes and misdemeanors"? Explain.

2. The impeachment of Bill Clinton is sometimes described as a power struggle between the legislative and executive branches. What evidence do you find for this point of view in the draft articles of impeachment? Explain.

3. How did President Richard Nixon's resignation in 1974 influence Congress to impeach President Clinton? Explain your answer.

Checks and Balances

Washington's Inauguration The chancellor of New York, Robert R. Livingston, in robes, administers the oath of office to the nation's first President.

Major Jack Downing, I must act in this case with energy and decision, you see the downfall of the party engine and corrupt monopoly !!

ORDER for the Removal of the Public Money deposited in the UNITED STATES BANK

Hurrah! General! if this don't beat skunkin. I'm a nigger; only see that var mint Nick how spry he is, he runs along like a Weatherfield Hog with an onion in his mouth.

The Downfall of Mother Bank Jackson waves his executive order for removing public money from the national bank, and its pillars fall on those who benefited from it. His decision helped make the presidency dominant over both Congress, which had created the bank, and the Supreme Court, that had ruled it was constitutional.

King Andrew the First This critical cartoon shows Jackson as a king holding a scepter and the veto while trampling the Constitution with one foot and the national bank with the other. ▶

THE INGENIOUS QUARTERBACK!

▲
Truman and the Senate Suggesting that Congress might drag its feet in approving the United Nations Charter that had been adopted in San Francisco in 1945, President Truman presses Senate leaders to act swiftly.

◀ **The Ingenious Quarterback** After the Supreme Court ruled that a number of New Deal bills were unconstitutional, President Franklin D. Roosevelt tried unsuccessfully to "reform" the Court (1937). Here Roosevelt (FDR), the quarterback, asks Congress, the referee, to let him add six "substitutes" to the Supreme Court team.

The Presidency Checked *The power of the presidency reached new heights by the early 1970s. However, the Constitution's checks and balances came into play when a House Judiciary Committee investigation of the Watergate affair charged President Richard Nixon (1969–1974) with obstruction of justice, abuse of power, and with contempt of Congress. As a result, Nixon resigned.*

Impeachment Hearings Members of the House Judiciary Committee hold hearings (1974) to find out how much Republican President Nixon knew about the cover-up of the burglary at the Democratic election head-quarters in the Watergate building.
▼

Barbara Jordan Television coverage of the hearings gave national recognition to the Representative from Texas as she displayed forcefulness and intelligence in her questioning of witnesses.

▲

Nixon Leaves Office Nixon signs a brave "thumbs up" to his
supporters after making his goodbye speech at the White House.
Daughter Tricia Nixon Cox and her husband Edward stand behind
him. Wife Pat precedes him.

Interest Groups and the Media

from

The Powers That Be

BY DAVID HALBERSTAM

*Franklin Roosevelt, President from 1933 to 1945, transformed the
power of both the press and the presidency by his adept handling
of the printed news media, particularly White House reporters,
and the new medium of radio. His continuing influence on
twentieth-century presidential relationships with the media
is evaluated in this excerpt from journalist and historian
David Halberstam's best-selling book,* The Powers That Be.

It was like a news explosion. The pace had been
so slow before Roosevelt, so relaxed and genteel.
Washington, after all, was not that big a **dateline**.[1] There
had been only a handful of reporters there who really
mattered and who covered national events, five or six of
them perhaps. They were all gentlemen **emulating**[2] the

---

[1] **dateline**—place of news. The city from which a news story originates, the
dateline, is, in many newspapers, the first word of a story.

[2] **emulating**—trying to equal or excel.

style of Richard Oulahan of *The New York Times* and J. Fred Essery of the Baltimore *Sun*, the **beau ideals**[3] of the time, very properly dressed, men who wore **fedoras**[4] and carried walking sticks. The walking sticks were symbolic, they were a sign of the more leisurely professions; after Franklin Roosevelt came there would be no more walking sticks. To their colleagues they were *Mister* Oulahan and *Mister* Essery. Mister Essery even wore a starched shirtfront. Croswell Bowen of International News Service had arrived in the late Twenties and he, new in town and much influenced by *The Front Page*,[5] had deliberately affected a style that was in part rumpled and in part seedy; but he had quickly gotten the message and soon was appearing with both a fedora and a walking stick. They were all men in their forties and fifties, it was not yet a young man's beat. They were the cream of a new crop of journalists, they covered the activities of dignitaries, and their clothes, as much as anything else, put some distance between them and other reporters, those who covered murders and other police stories. They were very deliberately making the profession more serious; why, [Herbert] Hoover himself was said to be personally fond of Oulahan, and later, while still President, attended Oulahan's funeral, a mark of great distinction for Oulahan. They all carried calling cards, they never rushed from one office to another; they knew all the people they spoke to by name and they as rarely as possible used the telephone, the telephone was a sign of being rushed, it seemed a mark of discourtesy. Besides, there was always time to visit news sources in person, the government was so small, there were so few sources of information. The State, Navy, and War Building housed the entire American

---

[3] **beau ideals**—French for "ideal gentlemen," models, fashionable men.

[4] **fedoras**—soft felt hats.

[5] *The Front Page* was a famous play about Chicago journalists, featuring sloppily dressed, wise-cracking, cynical reporters.

military and national security complex, such as it was. They would drive to the Ellipse[6] in the morning, parking their cars there, a good hundred yards away from the White House itself, complaining bitterly to each other how inconvenient it was all becoming with this new heavy traffic; then they began their rounds. The first stop was often the Interior Building, because it was usually good for a story on Indians. In the Twenties in Washington the Indian story was a big one, Indians were one of the few major concerns of the federal government. Then, often traveling as a small group, they would go on to the War Department Building. Secretary of State Kellogg saw them very regularly, though there were those who did not think Kellogg a particularly good source of information. Sometimes they saw General Pershing [commander of the U.S. Army] as well. Then they went to the White House and tried to see the President. There was no need for White House **credentials**[7] as such, everyone knew everyone else, if there was a new reporter his colleagues vouched for him. One reporter covered the entire executive branch in those days—the White House, State, War, Interior, Commerce—so if a colleague covered the Congress two men might make up the entire bureau. (Thirty years later ten or twelve reporters might be necessary to cover a comparable number of departments, and most of their work would be done by phone; there simply wasn't time for very much human contact.)

When journalists visited President Hoover they submitted their questions for him in writing. On occasion he **deigned**[8] to answer them. In writing, of course. Increasingly, as the weight of the Depression

---

[6] The Ellipse is a meadow-like park directly behind the White House grounds.

[7] **credentials**—photo identification badges now issued to White House reporters that permit them to enter the building.

[8] **deigned**—agreed in a condescending manner.

bore down on him, Hoover declined to respond at all. Indeed, his press secretary suggested on occasion that the reporters would do well not even to use the terms "financial crisis" and "unemployment" in their stories without checking with the White House press office. Some of them thought that bordered on censorship. Complaints were made and the White House backed down. Most of them were disappointed with Mr. Hoover. Before becoming President he had been a much-admired figure, a talented administrator with an international reputation for having brought food to a starving world after World War I. Washington journalists were in fact the very ones who had built his reputation, for, in truth, Herbert Hoover, outwardly stiff and formal, particularly as President, had been, before taking office, a very good source of news, very accessible, very manipulative, a very good all-around **leak.**[9] But Hoover had changed even before the Depression, when he ran for the presidency in 1928. It was as if he were a different and now more important man and such close contact with working reporters was below not just his dignity but that of his intended office. He was very good, it turned out, at outlining the flaws and weaknesses of government as long as someone else was in charge of the government.

As the Depression grew worse, Hoover had turned inward; he had been unable to deal with the terrifying turn of events. Immobilized politically by his fate, he grew hostile and **petulant.**[10] He blamed reporters for his problems and his diminished popularity, as if his hard times during the Depression were their fault and the economic chaos was primarily a public relations problem. He became obsessed with what was written about him, and punitive toward reporters. "Knowing that the newspapers made him, he assumes with equal ease they

---

[9] **leak**—secret, or at least unnamed, source of inside information for reporters.

[10] **petulant**—irritable.

can destroy him," wrote Paul Anderson, one of Washington's better reporters. There were more and more squabbles between the President and the press; on several minor occasions, such as when reporters wrote about a Marine guard being bitten by one of the dogs at Hoover's fishing camp, there were investigations launched to find out who their sources were. It was a bad time for the nation and a bad time for the President. The country was in economic collapse, and the entire nation waited to hear what Hoover was going to do. The President was largely silent. In his first year, he had held twenty-three press conferences and handed out eight press statements; in his last year as President, when the country most desperately wanted contact with him, wanted leadership and wanted a voice, he held only twelve press conferences and handed out twenty-six statements.

Franklin Roosevelt changed all that. He was the greatest newsmaker that Washington had ever seen. He came at a time when the society was ready for vast political and economic change, all of it enhancing the power of the President and the federal government, and he accelerated that change. The old order had collapsed, old institutions and old myths had failed; he would create the new order. In the new order, government would enter the everyday existence of almost all its citizens, regulating and adjusting their lives. Under him Washington became the focal point, it determined how people worked, how much they made, what they ate, where they lived. Before his arrival, the federal government was small and timid; by the time he died it reached everywhere, and as the government was everywhere, so Washington became the great dateline; as it was the source of power, so it was the source of news.

Roosevelt promised reporters two press conferences a week and, with astonishing regularity, he held to that: 337 in his first term, 374 in the second, 279 in the third.

United Press[11] carried *four* times as much Washington news in 1934 under him as it did in 1930 under Hoover; *one fourth* of all the world news on the Associated Press[12] wire in those days came from Washington. Suddenly everything was faster, the pace was quicker, there were so many more events, so many more government agencies, so many more sources, so many more stories. "You've got a mouthful now," Roosevelt had said as an early press conference was ending. "Better run." Run they did, there was no more time for walking sticks, no more time to put questions in writing, no more time for calling cards. The world had changed from one administration to another. Power in the wake of the Depression was waiting to be taken, and Franklin Roosevelt was going to take it, and those in the media were going to be his prime instrument.

... did he make news! Every day there were two or three stories coming out of the White House. He intended to make the whole federal government his, make it respond to his whim and vision; he did so, and in that struggle he became this century's prime **manipulator**[13] of the new and increasingly powerful modern media. Thirty and forty years later, politicians like John Kennedy and Lyndon Johnson would study how Franklin Roosevelt had handled the press. It was a textbook course in manipulation. The entire nation waited on him; if newsmen misread the rules and transgressed even slightly, he could come down hard and quickly, indeed quite brutally, on them. But the personality was secondary. Far more important was the fact that he was the best source in town. He understood exactly what journalists needed and when they needed it, and he understood from his Albany days that the

---

[11] United Press—a national news service.

[12] Associated Press—another major national news service that provided stories to newspapers.

[13] **manipulator**—skillful and shrewd controller.

very high public official who gives the greatest amount of information can dominate the story, often define the issue in question and thus dominate the government. Let no other government official dare try and take the play away from him and thwart his will. He was skilled at taking reporters behind the scenes, into the very heart of the mechanics of government, what was being done and why, explaining, in terms highly suitable and favorable to him, the working of the processes. He was thus divulging a staggering amount of information, all of it difficult to get by any other means, all of it sympathetic to him. And everything was happening so quickly that the reporters never had time to go to other sources; if they tried, they might make today's story better, but they would surely be beaten on tomorrow's. Roosevelt was as much teacher as spokesman, and he was always aware of every **nuance**,[14] of the constituency and mandate he was trying to create. He tried to shape every story. "If I were writing that story," he would often say, "I would write it along the lines . . ." Then he would dictate their **leads**.[15] In terms of public policy it was a tour de force.[16] Nothing like it had ever been seen before. "The best newspaperman who has ever been President of the United States," Heywood Broun called him. "The White House school of journalism," Raymond Clapper, one of the most distinguished of Washington reporters, labeled the entire operation.

It was, by contrast with previous operations, strikingly informal. There simply wasn't enough time for formality, and besides, Roosevelt's touch, that splendid patrician touch, required informality, without it he would have appeared a snob. In another time he might have seemed overbearing, but in the midst of the Depression, when the nation had lost its faith, it took

---

[14] **nuance**—delicate degree of difference.

[15] **leads**—opening sentences of news stories.

[16] tour de force—French term meaning "extraordinarily skillful act."

comfort in the fact that he was so sure of his destiny and his role. His destiny would become theirs. His confidence seemed inspiring. He knew the reporters by their first names and he laughed with them and exchanged small talk and, totally at ease with himself, he was totally at ease with them. He constantly assaulted the nation's newspaper publishers for their conservatism, which, given the greater class consciousness of the era, did not hurt him with working reporters. He went before the Daughters of the American Revolution and began his speech, "Fellow immigrants . . ." and the reporters covering him loved it. He even made up nicknames for them. Felix Belair of *The New York Times* became Butch because Roosevelt thought there ought to be someone named Butch at a paper as serious as the *Times*. His touch always seemed so sure. He was so confident of himself, so sure that he was the ablest man in the country to govern, so aware in his own **patrician**[17] way of his right to be doing what he was doing, that he seemed totally natural as President; it was a great art and he made it seem artless. It was astonishing in that era that someone so wellborn could have so intuitive a common touch; some friends thought it had come from the polio, that this had sensitized him and made him aware of the pain that others, less fortunate, suffered. It made him no less confident, and it made him far more aware.

He was a cripple. Those who covered him never wrote about it because Steve Early[18] asked them not to, and the White House photographers never took his photo in a wheelchair or on crutches because Early asked them not to; those were different days and reporters respected certain rights of the President. Felix Belair, working for *Time* [magazine] a few years later,

---

[17] **patrician**—aristocratic.

[18] Steve Early was Roosevelt's press secretary.

was with Roosevelt at Hyde Park when he had voted in the 1940 election. He had gone inside the voting booth and a lever had jammed. "This [expletive] thing doesn't work," came that rich familiar voice from the voting booth, and Belair had filed it and *Time* had printed the quote. Roosevelt was enraged—no one believed in those days that the President of the United States could lapse into profanity. Reporters had always shielded the public from presidential profanity and Roosevelt denied that he had been **blasphemous**.[19]

Nor did the journalists covering him think of Roosevelt as a cripple; he seemed to radiate such immense power and force, a kind of magnetic vitality. The first time that Felix Belair, then newly assigned by the *Times* to the White House, met Roosevelt was after a press conference in 1936. Steve Early, as was his **wont**[20] with new reporters, had waited until the conference was over and then he had brought the new man up to meet the President. The first thing that Belair noticed was the head, how massive and forceful it was, a head waiting for a great artist to sculpt it. Then the hand. The hand was enormous, like a Virginia ham, Belair thought, as it swallowed up his own hand. "Mister President," Early was saying, "do you know Felix Belair of *The New York Times?*" Then that voice, rich and powerful, so sure of itself, sweeping over Belair: "No. I don't believe I've had the pleasure, but I've read his stuff." Could it be more perfect? He even had the phrasing right, why, that was the way other newspapermen spoke to each other about their work, *I've read his stuff.* Just one of the boys. Whenever it suited him.

He was very good with the boys, the five or six or seven regulars who traveled with him on all trips, able to be one of them when he chose, even on occasion

---

[19] **blasphemous**—disrespectful of God.

[20] **wont**—custom.

playing poker with them. Once he had blown up at one of the regulars at a press conference, and he immediately realized that he had gone too far and come down too **imperiously**.[21] Later the reporter apologized for being a little sleepy because they had all been up until 4 A.M. playing poker. Poker, the President said, that sounded like a good idea, he hadn't played poker with them in a long time. He turned to Marvin McIntyre, his other press secretary, and told him to get together a buffet dinner, they would all play poker that night. So they played that night and Willard Edwards of the Chicago *Tribune* played and he was also a few drinks ahead of the others, and, as if carrying out the *Trib's* editorial opposition to Roosevelt, he raised every time the President raised. He did not do this very well, and Roosevelt kept winning the hands, but it did not deter Edwards. "Colonel McCormick's[22] money is better than any [expletive] New Deal money," he kept saying. McIntyre, watching, was shocked and made a signal to the other reporters to get Edwards out of there, but Roosevelt waved him off. He was taking the Colonel's money and he was in no hurry to get rid of the Colonel's man.

Roosevelt's hold on his press corps was very powerful. In part he was brilliant at the mechanics of their craft and they, like everyone else, were members of the society. He held their hopes in his hand just as he did those of their readers. The years of the Depression had been so bleak; reporters, like everyone else, had wanted a savior, wanted him to succeed, wanted the New Deal to work. It had rained heavily on inauguration day and there was mud everywhere but it had not dimmed their anticipation of the new era. At one point along the parade route Turner Catledge of the *Times* had

---

[21] **imperiously**—haughtily.

[22] McCormick was the conservative, Roosevelt-hating publisher of the Chicago *Tribune*.

looked down and seen a new dime. He had picked it up and said, "Now I know everything's going to be all right." Any symbol would do. So Roosevelt began with the benefit of the doubt and, indeed, more. He was also very skilled, once in office, at using peer pressure to keep reporters in line, isolating any journalist who asked too difficult a question, making him look ridiculous. There was a small group of regulars who sat in the front-row seats at all White House press conferences and who were totally Roosevelt's men. They laughed at every joke and pun; the others called them The Giggle Club. There was no doubt that the President used them effectively; not only would a potential **dissident**[23] feel the quick lash of the President's tongue, but he might also hear what seemed to be the laughter of his colleagues. When Bob Post of the *Times* asked, in 1937, whether the President was considering a third term, Roosevelt had answered, "Go sit in the corner and put on a dunce cap," and everyone had laughed. Another time, angered by the **isolationist**[24] writings of John O'Donnell of the New York *Daily News*, the President had awarded O'Donnell an Iron Cross. Once, when he was feuding with [Washington editor] Arthur Krock of the *Times* and Felix Belair asked a question he did not like, Roosevelt had answered, "I bet little Arthur sat up all night framing that one." Much laughter. Another time, when Belair seemed to doze off at a press conference while Roosevelt was going through a tirade against fat-cat publishers, a favorite theme, the President had exploded "Belair! I don't care what paper you represent! You're here on my **sufferance**[25] and when you're here you will take notes!" It was a shattering moment for Belair, the President of the United States shouting at him. There were not many

---

[23] **dissident**—opponent.

[24] **isolationist**—against active involvement in world affairs.

[25] **sufferance**—consent; permission.

moments like that but there were enough to remind the regulars who was in charge, informal or not, family atmosphere or not. Once, after the 1942 election, Richard Harkness, then with United Press, had written in his overnight story that Roosevelt had voted the straight Democratic ticket. The next day Harkness was sitting with other reporters when an enraged Roosevelt sought him out. "You have destroyed the secrecy of the ballot! How dare you announce that I voted in any way? How dare you say I voted straight Democratic or anything else?"

But those moments were the exception. It was a reporter's dream; there was so much energy, so much action, so much access. Roosevelt had an **intuitive**[26] grasp of the way the press worked, could be worked. His sense of timing was **impeccable**;[27] he once told [movie star] Orson Welles that there were two great actors in America at that moment. Welles, he said, was the other one. Besides, the rhythm of the times, the great inventions and the changing shape of society, were working to centralize power. The coming of radio and airplanes was breaking down regionalism and making the nation, in a clearer sense, one. Radio was a network; one man's voice was heard across the entire country. Issues became national rather than **parochial**[28] and regional. In the old era Washington was filled with journalists who covered regional issues for their regional papers; when the Roosevelt era was over Washington was filled with reporters who were often highly trained specialists who wrote of national implications for the entire country. The speed of decisions was becoming faster and faster and, as it did, local governments simply could not keep up with the growing power and

---

[26] **intuitive**—instinctive.
[27] **impeccable**—flawless.
[28] **parochial**—local.

affluence of the federal government. The federal government's taxing power increased as its **mandate**[29] increased, and as its taxing power increased, so did its real power. Technology was bringing the central state a longer and more powerful reach. The central state could reach areas previously isolated. More, it could perform functions, deliver services, and make judgments inconceivable in another era.

Nor was this an isolated phenomenon. It was happening throughout the world. In Germany and in the Soviet Union, powerful, highly centralized governments had taken power, and their very rise strengthened the coming of the centralized government in America. Highly centralized **totalitarian**[30] states were deeply threatening; if power was more clearly centralized elsewhere, might not a democracy prove vulnerable, might not, in an age of increasingly swift and destructive bombers and other weapons, democracy be too slow, too awkward? So the coming of totalitarian states strengthened the American presidency, giving the President leverage which he used not just against the **adversary**[31] states but against the American public, Congress, and press, arguing the needs of national security. Similarly, as the peacetime Roosevelt years ended and World War II began, the focus was to change from domestic issues, about which the Congress was informed and felt itself equal, to foreign policy and national security, where Congress felt itself ignorant and clumsy and thus inevitably **subservient**.[32]

All this began in the thirties, the arrival of new forces that were to make the American presidency for some forty years almost unchallenged in its power, and

---

[29] **mandate**—authorization from citizens.
[30] **totalitarian**—undemocratic; dictatorial.
[31] **adversary**—enemy.
[32] **subservient**—submissive.

it all began under Franklin Roosevelt. A lesser man, a more modest man, might have shrunk from all these possibilities and implications as he took office, but Roosevelt welcomed them; he welcomed the chance to change things, to expand the powers of the government, and he knew immediately how to create his own new mandate.

He was, of course, subtly but quite consciously elevating the importance of the press. If he wanted direct access to their readers, then they had to have direct access to him. He was more often than not going directly to the media rather than to the Congress with information; and he put more energy into his press relations than into his congressional ones. There was a changing institutional balance. If on occasion print reporters were angered by his increased use of and chumminess with radio reporters, then people in the Congress and some Democratic Party politicians were irritated by the fact that he seemed to court media people in general more than he did them. He simply needed the Congress and the party structure less.

As he used the media more often and more directly, they became more influential; they became more and more architects of the national agenda, making more decisions on what the great issues were rather than just responding to the decisions of others. The press corps was becoming a different, more serious, and better informed body. Reporters became, with their greater role in the Roosevelt years, more influential and more prestigious around town, more sought after; similarly, as the stories became more serious and more complicated, the people writing them became better qualified, better educated, and more serious.

In those early Roosevelt years reporters like Catledge and Belair, who had covered the Congress in the old era, could almost feel the tide changing, the

Congress becoming weaker; no one on the Hill[33] even seemed to know it was happening. One moment in 1937 seemed to crystallize it for Belair: the President was at Warm Springs and he had been driving around in his manually operated car and he had stopped where the reporters were gathered, for an **impromptu**[34] outdoor, curbstone press conference. The setting seemed to emphasize the informality of it, the President driving up in front of waiting reporters, teasing them—*Are you all right? You probably want something from me to write about?* Then he had quickly gotten down to business. There was a major Congressional struggle on at the time on the question of devaluing the dollar; the President wanted the devaluation and big business in general opposed it. The news had come in that day that the Senate had voted for devaluation, which did not surprise Belair. What did surprise him was Roosevelt's tone. He was boundlessly full of himself that day, more so than usual, and he seemed exalted by the triumph. "This proves," he said, "that the Senate of the United States cannot be bought." Belair was scribbling down the words, but even as he did, he was thinking, *Who ever said that it could be bought?* It was the colossal arrogance of it, it symbolized to Belair how completely Roosevelt had taken over the town, how personal an instrument of his will he had made the office, it was his possession and so was everything else in Washington. It was as if it were now *his* Senate. If the Senate responded as he wanted, it was a good Senate, otherwise it was a bad one. It often seemed in those years, Belair thought, as if a new kind of politics had come into existence, so forceful and all-encompassing was the power of the President. He could reach past anything that stood in

---

[33] Hill—Capitol Hill, site of the Capitol building that houses Congress.

[34] **impromptu**—offhand; unrehearsed.

his way, the opposition party, the Congress, his own party, the Supreme Court.

Part of it was the special quality of the moment; the Depression gave Roosevelt vast political freedom and also permitted him, as a media figure, to play exactly the kind of role in exactly the type of theater he wanted— Roosevelt the friend of the common man, his opponents the friends of the old, discredited, **exploitative**[35] order. There was also one large new ingredient in the political composition of the country and that was radio. Roosevelt had made radio his own personal instrument and had changed permanently the institutional balance of politics. Radio had been a powerful force in the country for almost a decade; by the time of his inauguration it was already the most important means of entertainment in the country and it represented a means of merchandising that was beginning to rival and even threaten magazine advertising. But it had been scarcely used as a political instrument. Herbert Hoover, in desperate political trouble, needing all the assets he could muster, had not deigned to use radio. Men of his generation looked at it with contempt. It was beneath their dignity. Hoover's rare broadcasts had been awkward, stilted, **pedantic**,[36] words written and spoken in governmentese.[37] Rather than humanizing the President, they had merely confirmed the impression of an uncaring man in a distant office. Yet the instrument was there and sooner or later some shrewd politician was going to make a powerful national connection.

The first broadcast had been made in 1920 and the public response had been quick and enthusiastic; by 1922 there were some 220 radio stations in the country. The sets themselves, simple models, sold for about $10.

---

[35] **exploitative**—abusive by taking advantage of others.

[36] **pedantic**—dull; overly scholarly.

[37] governmentese—the formal, legal, often overly complicated language of government.

Stores were not able to keep them in stock, manufacturers had to rush forward their orders. By 1923 there were already 2.5 million sets in the country. Millions of Americans had made radio the focal point of their households, scheduling their day around their favorite programs. When "Amos 'n' Andy"[38] was on the air, the nation simply stopped all its other business and listened. When Pepsodent sponsored "Amos 'n' Andy" its sales tripled in just a few weeks. The way was clear. Those companies which were highly dependent on popular taste, like toothpaste and cigarettes, saw the light; by 1931 the American Tobacco Company spent $19 million to advertise Lucky Strike on radio. Was it surprising then, with audiences and sales like that, that Franklin Roosevelt, free of charge, was soon selling himself and the New Deal on radio? He was the first great American radio voice. For most Americans of this generation, their first memory of politics would be of sitting by a radio and hearing *that* voice, strong, confident, totally at ease. If he was going to speak, the idea of doing something else was unthinkable. If they did not yet have a radio, they walked the requisite several hundred yards to the home of a more fortunate neighbor who did. It was in the most direct sense the government reaching out and touching the citizen, bringing Americans into the political process and focusing their attention on the presidency as the source of good. Roosevelt was the first professional of the art. He had practiced for it as governor of New York. The first time he had used radio as President he had turned to Carleton Smith of NBC, the one radio man allowed in the room, and had said, "You'll never have any trouble with me, I'm an old hand at this." Which he was. Smith (whom NBC had chosen to replace Herluf Provenson because the Roosevelt people thought Provenson was

---

[38] "Amos 'n' Andy"—a popular radio comedy show.

too close to Hoover) had a stopwatch that Roosevelt always used to time himself. He called it "that famous watch." Smith was impressed by Roosevelt's ability to stay almost exactly within the prescribed time limits. When it was over he would always turn to Smith and ask: How did it go? Was I repetitious? Were there any lapses? There rarely were; it was a **consummately**[39] professional performance.

Most Americans in the previous 160 years had never even seen a President; now almost all of them were hearing him, *in their own homes*. It was literally and figuratively electrifying. Because he was President he had access to the airwaves any time he wanted, when he wanted. Indeed, because he was such a good performer, because his messages so bound the nation, the networks wanted him on more often, regularly, perhaps once a week (an offer he shrewdly turned down, aware of the danger of overexposure, telling a network official that people cannot stand the repetition of the highest note on the scale for very long). "You guys want him to do everything," Steve Early, Roosevelt's press secretary, once told Carleton Smith. "I don't want the Boss to do very much. We want to conserve him."

He spoke in an informal manner, his speeches were scripted not to be read in newspapers but to be heard aloud. He worked carefully on them in advance, often spending several days on a speech, reading the words aloud, working on the rhythm and the **cadence**,[40] getting the feel of them down right. When aides questioned the immense amount of time he devoted to just one speech, Roosevelt said that it was probably the most important thing he would do all week. He had an intuitive sense of radio cadence. Unlike most people, who speeded up their normal speech pattern on radio,

---

[39] **consummately**—completely, thoroughly.
[40] **cadence**—flow of sounds.

Roosevelt deliberately slowed his down. He was never in a rush. He had often memorized a speech before he began, and so he seemed infinitely confident, never seemed to stumble. The patterns of the speech were conversational. His very first words reflected his ease: "My friends," he began. *My friends.* That was it, they were his friends. Nor were they a passive audience. At that desperate moment in American history the American people were not cool, not aloof, they needed him and they wanted him to succeed; what could be more stirring than to be told by that man with that rich assured voice that the only thing they had to fear was fear itself.

It was all so personal. This was not some distant government official talking in governmentese, this was a voice connected to a warm human being—he knew them, he had visited them. He spoke of his wife and his children, even his dog. Some thirty-five years later an astonishing number of Americans who did not remember the names of the dogs of Harry Truman, Dwight Eisenhower, and John Kennedy, remembered the name of Franklin Roosevelt's dog because he had spoken with them about Fala, *my little dog Fala,* about Fala's Irish being up over Republican criticism. It was an awesome display of mastery. It was as if sitting in the studio he could visualize his audience sitting around their radios in their homes, and he spoke not to the microphone but to those homes. If it was very hot in Washington he might turn to an aide and ask, over the open mike, for a glass of water, and apologize to his audience, and that too **humanized**[41] him, the President needed a glass of water. His touch was perfect. Often, when the speech was over, because newsreels were becoming a bigger and bigger factor in American life, Roosevelt would then repeat vital parts of the speech for a newsreel

[41] **humanized**—made him likeable.

camera. But the camera was not allowed in to film the broadcast itself; it was simply too noisy in those days.

Nearly 50 million Americans listened to most of his speeches. They were in a real sense his own captive audience. Not by chance was he the first three-term and then four-term President in the nation's history, rising above tradition, above opposition party, above his own party's will. (No longer did politicians need the party to raise a crowd. Now the radio did it. Yet few professional politicians of the day understood radio or how to use it. Carleton Smith of NBC tried to do a program with members of Roosevelt's Cabinet and had a terrible problem. Jim Farley, the Postmaster General and ablest professional politician of his generation, simply could not pronounce the word "with." It always came out "wit," making Farley seem like a hack.) Thus did Franklin Roosevelt outdistance even his own party. He had changed the institutional balance[42] and he changed the nature of the presidency; from now on it was a personalized office, less distant from the average American. Until March 1933, through a world war and a Great Depression, the White House had employed only one person to handle the incoming mail. Herbert Hoover had received, for example, some 40 letters a day. After Franklin Roosevelt arrived and began to make his radio speeches, the average was closer to 4,000 letters a day.

The White House reporters, of course, resented the coming of radio, and even more, the coming of the first radio correspondents. Never mind that radio inevitably **whetted**[43] interest in government and thus increased readership, never mind that radio would act as a kind of monitor and force journalism to improve, ending the

---

[42] institutional balance—balance between the branches and levels of government.
[43] **whetted**—increased.

Hearst[44] style of reporting, what was at stake was turf. Suddenly there was a new kind of reporter around, reporters who, to the eye of the print traditionalists, weren't reporters at all. They were pretty boys with slick voices and worse, they seemed to have stunningly quick access to vast audiences. Carleton Smith of NBC was the first radio correspondent at the White House. His job was to place a microphone in front of the President and tap Roosevelt on the shoulder when the network hookup was ready. NBC in those early days was the dominant company. Poor Bob Trout, the first CBS man, had to stand outside the door. The first time that Roosevelt saw a CBS microphone he asked, "CBS? What's that?" But CBS gradually got into the act. John Charles Daly succeeded Trout. Daly was not so much a correspondent in the early days as he was a special-events man; he was supposed to cover the launching of ships and to help broadcast concerts by the Army Band on Mondays and the Marine Band on Wednesdays. Daly—smooth, strikingly handsome, with a rich voice— inspired even more resentment among the print reporters, particularly from Belair of the *Times* and Walter Trohan, the feisty correspondent of the Chicago *Tribune*. Trohan in particular did not like radio and he especially did not like John Charles Daly. "That man's no reporter," he used to complain to his colleagues. "He's never worked in a city room. He's never covered a story. *I think he's an actor.*" What makes you think he's not a reporter? Belair asked. "Because reporters play poker when they're not working and that man is off in the woods practicing lines from Shakespeare, listening to his own voice," Trohan answered.

---

[44] Hearst—William Randolph Hearst, publisher of newspapers across America that specialized in sensationalized journalism.

Daly, of course, was not shy. He had his job and part of it was to push for access. That part was made easier by the growing size of the audiences; no one had to tell Franklin Roosevelt where people gathered. Gradually the status of Carleton Smith and Daly changed; correspondents they wanted to be, correspondents they were. Soon they rode in the third car in presidential caravans. In those days position was based on circulation; the [national news] wire services were in the first car; the specials, men like Belair and Trohan, in the second; and the networks in the third. That was not good enough for Daly and he kept arguing that the networks in status were in fact equal to the wire services. That was a staggering presumption for the times and at first not only did the print reporters resist it, but more important Steve Early refused to accept it. But Daly persisted; on occasion, he argued, the networks had a greater circulation than the wires, although in sum the wires had a basic circulation that was higher. But certainly more people heard CBS than read the *Times*. Finally Early, after consultation with his boss, agreed, and at the start of a presidential trip, Early changed the rating system, putting the networks in the second car. As they all rushed to their cars Daly and Smith found Walter Trohan in the second car. . . . Trohan told Daly, "this is our car." Not any more, it wasn't. Daly summoned Early, who forced the Chicago *Tribune* and *The New York Times* to car three. When Felix Belair complained mildly to Early later, the press secretary apologized. "It's not that we like them better," he said. Radio had arrived.

QUESTIONS TO CONSIDER

1. What was the relationship between news reporters and the President before Franklin Roosevelt took office in 1933?

2. What techniques did Franklin Roosevelt use to gain control of the news and influence the press corps?

3. Why was Roosevelt's confidence in himself and his easy relationship with reporters so important to the country during the 1930s?

4. What world events of the 1930s worked to increase the power of the United States presidency? In what ways did Roosevelt encourage this trend?

5. In what ways did Roosevelt's use of radio change politics and the presidency?

The Checkers Speech

BY SENATOR RICHARD M. NIXON

Early in his political career, Richard Nixon demonstrated a powerful ability to use the media to dodge political disaster. Nixon, a first-term U.S. senator from California, had been picked at the 1952 Republican convention as General Dwight Eisenhower's vice presidential running mate. His candidacy was jeopardized, however, by accusations that his political career was being financed from a fund created by wealthy supporters. On September 23, 1952, Nixon used the new medium of television to deliver his "Checkers speech." (Checkers, a dog given to his two daughters by a political admirer, appeared along with the rest of the Nixon family in the televised speech.) The positive popular response to the talk convinced Eisenhower to keep Nixon as his running mate, and Nixon served as Vice President for eight years.

My Fellow Americans, I come before you tonight as a candidate for the vice presidency and as a man whose honesty and integrity has been questioned.

Now, the usual political thing to do when charges are made against you is to either ignore them or to deny them without giving details. I believe we have had enough of that in the United States, particularly with the present administration[1] in Washington, D.C.

To me, the office of the vice presidency of the United States is a great office, and I feel that the people have got to have confidence in the integrity of the men who run for that office and who might attain it.

I have a theory, too, that the best and only answer to a smear or an honest misunderstanding of the facts is to tell the truth. And that is why I am here tonight. I want to tell you my side of the case.

I am sure that you have read the charges, and you have heard it, that I, Senator Nixon, took $18,000 from a group of my supporters.

Now, was that wrong? And let me say that it was wrong. I am saying it, incidentally, that it was wrong, just not illegal, because it isn't a question of whether it was legal or illegal, that isn't enough. The question is, was it morally wrong? I say that it was morally wrong if any of that $18,000 went to Senator Nixon, for my personal use. I say that it was morally wrong if it was secretly given and secretly handled.

And I say that it was morally wrong if any of the contributors got special favors for the contributions that they made.

And to answer those questions let me say this—not a cent of the $18,000 or any other money of that type ever went to me for my personal use. Every penny of it was used to pay for political expenses that I did not think should be charged to the taxpayers of the United States.

---

[1] present administration—that of the opposing party led by Democratic President Harry Truman.

It was not a secret fund. As a matter of fact, when I was on "Meet the Press"[2]—some of you may have seen it last Sunday—Peter Edson came up to me after the program, and he said, "Dick, what about this fund we hear about?" And I said, "Well, there is no secret about it. Go out and see Dana Smith who was the administrator of the fund," and I gave him his address. And I said you will find that the purpose of the fund simply was to defray political expenses that I did not feel should be charged to the government.

And third, let me point out, and I want to make this particularly clear, that no contributor to this fund, no contributor to any of my campaigns, has ever received any consideration that he would not have received as an ordinary constituent.

I just don't believe in that, and I can say that never, while I have been in the Senate of the United States, as far as the people that contributed to this fund are concerned, have I made a telephone call to an agency, nor have I gone down to an agency on their behalf.

And the records will show that—the records which are in the hands of the [Truman] administration.

. . . And I would like to tell you this evening that just an hour ago we received an independent audit of this entire fund. I suggested to Governor Sherman Adams, who is the chief of staff of the Eisenhower campaign, that an independent audit and legal report be obtained, and I have that audit in my hand.

It is an audit made by the Price Waterhouse & Co. firm, and the legal opinion by Gibson, Dunn, & Crutcher, lawyers in Los Angeles, the biggest law firm, and incidentally, one of the best ones in Los Angeles.

I am proud to report to you tonight that this audit and legal opinion is being forwarded to General Eisenhower and I would like to read to you the opinion

---

[2] "Meet the Press"—an influential political TV show that focused on interviews with newsmakers.

that was prepared by Gibson, Dunn, & Crutcher, based on all the **pertinent**[3] laws, and statutes, together with the audit report prepared by the certified public accountants:

"It is our conclusion that Senator Nixon did not obtain any financial gain from the collection and disbursement of the funds by Dana Smith; that Senator Nixon did not violate any federal or state law by reason of the operation of the fund; and that neither the portion of the fund paid by Dana Smith directly to third persons, nor the portion paid to Senator Nixon, to reimburse him for office expenses, constituted income in a sense which was either reportable or taxable as income under income tax laws."

Signed—Gibson, Dunn, & Crutcher, by Elmo Conley

* * *

That is not Nixon speaking, but it is an independent audit which was requested because I want the American people to know all the facts and I am not afraid of having independent people go in and check the facts, and that is exactly what they did.

But then I realized that there are still some who may say, and rightly so—and let me say that I recognize that some will continue to smear regardless of what the truth may be—but that there has been understandably, some honest misunderstanding on this matter, and there are some that will say, "Well, maybe you were able, Senator, to fake the thing. How can we believe what you say— after all, is there a possibility that maybe you got some sums in cash? Is there a possibility that you might have feathered your own nest?" And so now, what I am going to do—and incidentally this is unprecedented in the history of American politics—I am going at this time to

---

[3] **pertinent**—relevant.

give to this television and radio audience a complete financial history, everything I have earned, everything I have spent and everything I own, and I want you to know the facts.

I will have to start early. I was born in 1913. Our family was one of modest circumstances, and most of my early life was spent in a store out in East Whittier. It was a grocery store, one of those family enterprises.

The only reason we were able to make it go was because my mother and dad had five boys, and we all worked in the store. I worked my way through college, and, to a great extent, through law school. And then in 1940, probably the best thing that ever happened to me happened. I married Pat who is sitting over here.

We had a rather difficult time after we were married, like so many of the young couples who might be listening to us. I practiced law. She continued to teach school.

Then, in 1942, I went into the service. Let me say that my service record was not a particularly unusual one. I went to the South Pacific. I guess I'm entitled to a couple of battle stars. I got a couple of letters of commendation. But I was just there when the bombs were falling. And then I returned. I returned to the United States, and in 1946, I ran for Congress. When we came out of the war—Pat and I—Pat during the war had worked as a stenographer, and in a bank, and as an economist for a government agency—and when we came out, the total of our savings, from both my law practice, her teaching and all the time I was in the war, the total for that entire period was just less than $10,000—every cent of that, incidentally, was in government bonds—well, that's where we start, when I go into politics.

Now, whatever I earned since I went into politics—well, here it is. I jotted it down. Let me read the notes.

First of all, I have had my salary as a Congressman and as a Senator.

Second, I have received a total in this past six years of $1,600 from estates which were in my law firm at the time that I severed my connection with it. And, incidentally, as I said before, I have not engaged in any legal practice, and have not accepted any fees from business that came into the firm after I went into politics.

I have made an average of approximately $1,500 a year from nonpolitical speaking engagements and lectures.

And then, unfortunately, we have inherited little money. Pat sold her interest in her father's estate for $3,000, and I inherited $1,500 from my grandfather. We lived rather modestly.

For four years we lived in an apartment in Parkfairfax, Alexandria, Virginia. The rent was $80 a month. And we saved for a time when we could buy a house. Now that was what we took in.

What did we do with this money? What do we have today to show for it? This will surprise you because it is so little, I suppose, as standards generally go of people in public life.

First of all, we've got a house in Washington, which cost $41,000 and on which we owe $20,000. We have a house in Whittier, California, which cost $13,000 and on which we owe $3,000. My folks are living there at the present time.

I have just $4,000 in life insurance, plus my GI policy which I have never been able to convert, and which will run out in two years.

I have no life insurance whatever on Pat. I have no life insurance on our two youngsters, Patricia and Julie.

I own a 1950 Oldsmobile car. We have our furniture. We have no stocks and bonds of any type. We have no interest, direct or indirect, in any business. Now that is what we have. What do we owe?

Well, in addition to the mortgages, the $20,000 mortgage on the house in Washington and the $10,000 mortgage on the house in Whittier, I owe $4,000 to the Riggs Bank in Washington D.C. with an interest at 4 percent.

I owe $3,500 to my parents, and the interest on that loan, which I pay regularly, because it is a part of the savings they made through the years they were working so hard—I pay regularly 4 percent interest. And then I have a $500 loan, which I have on my life insurance. Well, that's about it. That's what we have. And that's what we owe. It isn't very much.

But Pat and I have the satisfaction that every dime that we have got is honestly ours.

I should say this, that Pat doesn't have a mink coat. But she does have a respectable Republican cloth coat, and I always tell her she would look good in anything.

One other thing I should probably tell you, because if I don't they will probably be saying this about me, too. We did get something, a gift, after the election.

A man down in Texas heard Pat on the radio mention that our two youngsters would like to have a dog, and, believe it or not, the day we left before this campaign trip we got a message from Union Station in Baltimore, saying they had a package for us. We went down to get it. You know what it was?

It was a little cocker spaniel dog, in a crate that he had sent all the way from Texas, black and white, spotted, and our little girl Tricia, the six-year-old, named it Checkers.

And you know, the kids, like all kids, loved the dog, and I just want to say this, right now, that regardless of what they say about it, we are going to keep it.

It isn't easy to come before a nation-wide audience and bare your life, as I have done. But I want to say some things before I conclude, that I think most of you will agree on.

Mr. Mitchell, the chairman of the Democratic National Committee,[4] made this statement that if a man couldn't afford to be in the United States Senate, he shouldn't run for Senate. And I just want to make my position clear.

I don't agree with Mr. Mitchell when he says that only a rich man should serve his government in the United States Senate or Congress. I don't believe that represents the thinking of the Democratic Party, and I know it doesn't represent the thinking of the Republican Party.

I believe that it's fine that a man like Governor Stevenson,[5] who inherited a fortune from his father, can run for President. But I also feel that it is essential in this country of ours that a man of modest means can also run for President, because, you know—remember Abraham Lincoln—you remember what he said—"God must have loved the common people, he made so many of them. " . . .

Now let me say this: I know this is not the last of the smears. In spite of my explanation tonight, other smears will be made. Others have been made in the past. And the purpose of the smears, I know, is this, to silence me, to make me let up.

Well, they just don't know who they are dealing with. I'm going to tell you this: I remember in the dark days of the Hiss[6] trial some of the same columnists, some of the same radio commentators who are attacking me now and misrepresenting my position, were violently

---

[4] chairman of the Democratic National Committee—person responsible for coordinating election campaigns for the Democratic Party. Nixon, a Republican, is accusing Mitchell and the Democratic Party of believing that only rich men should be senators.

[5] Governor Stevenson—Adlai Stevenson, the governor of Illinois, was the Democratic presidential candidate in 1952.

[6] Hiss—Alger Hiss, an employee of the State Department investigated in the late 1940s by Congress for alleged spy activities and Communist leanings. As a congressman from California at the time, Nixon made a name for himself by serving on the House committee that investigated Hiss.

opposing me at the time I was after Alger Hiss. But I continued to fight because I knew I was right, and I can say to this great television and radio audience that I have no apologies to the American people for my part in putting Alger Hiss where he is today. And as far as this is concerned, I intend to continue to fight.

Why do I feel so deeply? Why do I feel that in spite of the smears, the misunderstanding, the necessity for a man to come up here and bare his soul? And I want to tell you why.

Because, you see, I love my country. And I think my country is in danger. And I think the only man that can save America at this time is the man that's running for President on my ticket, Dwight Eisenhower.

You say, why do I think it is in danger? And I say look at the record. Seven years of the Truman-Acheson[7] administration, and what's happened? Six hundred million people lost to Communists.[8]

And a war in Korea in which we have lost 117,000 American casualties, and I say that those in the State Department that made the mistakes which caused that war and which resulted in those losses should be kicked out of the State Department just as fast as we can get them out of there.

And let me say that I know Mr. Stevenson won't do that because he defends the Truman policy, and I know that Dwight Eisenhower will do that, and he will give America the leadership that it needs.

Take the problem of corruption. You have read about the mess in Washington. Mr. Stevenson can't clean it up because he was picked by the man, Truman, under whose administration the mess was made.

You wouldn't trust the man who made the mess to clean it up. That is Truman. And by the same token you can't trust the man who was picked by the man who

---

[7] Dean Acheson was President Truman's secretary of state.

[8] Nixon primarily refers to the Communist takeover of China in 1949.

made the mess to clean it up and that's Stevenson. And so I say, Eisenhower who owes nothing to Truman, nothing to the big city bosses—he is the man who can clean up the mess in Washington. . . .

And I say that the only man who can lead us into this fight to rid the government of both those who are Communists and those who have corrupted this government is Eisenhower, because General Eisenhower, you can be sure, recognizes the problem, and knows how to handle it.

Let me say this, finally. This evening I want to read to you just briefly excerpts from a letter that I received, a letter, which after all this is over, no one can take away from us. It reads as follows:

"Dear Senator Nixon,

Since I am only 19 years of age, I can't vote in this presidential election,[9] but believe me if I could, you and General Eisenhower would certainly get my vote. My husband is in the Fleet Marines in Korea. He is in the front lines. And we have a two-month-old son he has never seen. And I feel confident that with great Americans like you and General Eisenhower in the White House, lonely Americans like myself will be united with their loved ones now in Korea. I only pray to God that you won't be too late. Enclosed is a small check to help you with your campaign. Living on $85 a month it is all I can do."

Folks, it is a check for $10, and it is one that I shall never cash. And let me just say this: We hear a lot about prosperity these days, but I say why can't we have prosperity built on peace, rather than prosperity built on war? Why can't we have prosperity and an honest government in Washington, D.C. at the same time?

---

[9] The national age limit for voting was not reduced from 21 to 18 until 1968.

Believe me, we can. And Eisenhower is the man that can lead the crusade to bring us that kind of prosperity.

And now, finally, I know that you wonder whether or not I am going to stay on the Republican ticket or resign. Let me say this: I don't believe that I ought to quit, because I am not a quitter. And, incidentally, Pat is not a quitter. After all, her name is Patricia Ryan and she was born on St. Patrick's Day, and you know the Irish never quit.

But the decision, my friends, is not mine. I would do nothing that would harm the possibilities of Dwight Eisenhower to become President of the United States. And for that reason I am submitting to the Republican National Committee tonight through this television broadcast the decision which it is theirs to make. Let them decide whether my position on the ticket will help or hurt. And I am going to ask you to help them decide. Wire and write the Republican National Committee whether you think I should stay on or whether I should get off. And whatever their decision, I will abide by it.

But let me just say this last word. Regardless of what happens, I am going to continue this fight. I am going to campaign up and down America until we drive the crooks and the Communists and those that defend them out of Washington, and remember, folks, Eisenhower is a great man. Folks, he is a great man, and a vote for Eisenhower is a vote for what is good for America.

QUESTIONS TO CONSIDER

1. What answers does Richard Nixon give to the charges against him? Which seem most effective to you? Why?

2. Why did Nixon point out that his wife Pat had a "Republican cloth coat" and not a mink coat?

3. Why does Nixon refer to Checkers in his speech?

4. Today, do politicians' careers depend on their skills with the media? Support your answer with examples.

from

Jesse Jackson & the Politics of Race

BY THOMAS H. LANDESS AND
RICHARD M. QUINN

No African American has ever served as President of the United States, but the Reverend Jesse Jackson received significant support during presidential races in 1984 and 1988. His 1984 campaign won three-and-a-half million votes, registered over one million voters, and helped the Democratic party regain control of the Senate in 1986. In 1988, he won seven million votes, and his campaign registered two million new voters. The following excerpt describes the announcement of his candidacy for the Democratic presidential nomination in 1984.

November 3, 1983

Jesse Jackson rose to the podium at the Washington Convention Hall. Twenty-five hundred supporters cheered wildly. He raised his heavy lidded eyes and gazed directly into the bright television lights. He had called many press conferences over the years, but this one was different. He was a little nervous at first, his voice unsteady, but he quickly lost himself in his delivery. After a moment, only the sweat gleaming on his forehead suggested the tension within.

The political rally/press conference had been scheduled by Jackson to end a well-orchestrated period of speculation on whether the forty-two-year-old civil rights leader would run for the Democratic presidential nomination and thereby become the first black to conduct a presidential campaign since Shirley Chisholm, a former congresswoman from Brooklyn, who ran in 1972. A symbolic gesture of continuity, Ms. Chisholm preceded Jackson to the podium and introduced him to the crowd.

"I am announcing today," he spoke slowly at first, with a choppy emphasis on unaccented syllables, "that I am a candi-*date* for presi-*dent.*" The 2,500 cheerleaders gathered before the former star college quarterback burst into whoops and applause and the familiar chant *Run, Jesse, Run.*

Soon Jackson was caught up in the rhythm of his audience, his congregation, and he let them have a forty-five-minute sermon, a record length in the age of television for a candidacy announcement. "This is not about one person running," he said, "it's about 10,000 running." He was offering his candidacy to "help restore a moral tone, a redemptive spirit and a sensitivity to the poor and the dispossessed of the nation."

Jackson spent some of his time **skewering**[1] Ronald Reagan. He said Reagan's first four years in office had given not statesmanship or leadership but "showmanship and acting." Sounding somewhat like a populist

---

[1] **skewering**—criticizing.

candidate from an earlier era, Jackson accused Reagan and the Republicans of following a "pro-rich, pro-aristocratic, pro-agribusiness,[2] pro-military and pro-big business" policy that had abandoned the government's obligation to the poor.

But Jackson reserved his biggest guns for the Democrats. He said leadership of the Democratic party had been "too silent and too passive" while Reagan was tormenting the poor. And he said that none of the white men running for President offered the proper alternative to Reagan. "There is a gap," he said, "between the announced candidates and the masses."

Again Jackson referred to his Rainbow Coalition of minorities. And he said that the minorities he represented could do without the Democratic party "but they cannot do without us. We are necessary. We will assert ourselves. Our minds have spoken." Then finally he defined his proposal for a **coalition**.[3] He insisted that the Jackson campaign was not for blacks only but included "women, Hispanics, workers, Indians, Chinese, Europeans—we must come together and form a rainbow coalition."

Then stretching his hands to the heavens, in the dramatic style of a Southern Baptist preacher, he cried out: "These hands" (repeating the phrase several times as the crowd roared its approval). "These hands that picked cotton can pick the next President of the United States."

The moment was golden. Even on his best Saturday mornings at the headquarters of Operation PUSH,[4] Jackson had never delivered himself better. For the purpose of launching his campaign, everything was perfect.

---

[2] pro-agribusiness—in support of large farming businesses. Jackson sees agribusiness as an enemy of ordinary people.

[3] **coalition**—loose organization of many groups of people.

[4] PUSH—People United to Serve Humanity, a Chicago-based organization founded by Jackson to promote the well-being of minorities.

QUESTIONS TO CONSIDER

1. What is the meaning of Jackson's comment: "This is not about one person running, it's about 10,000 running"?

2. Why did Jackson call his followers "The Rainbow Coalition"?

3. The Presidents of the United States have all been white men, and all but one have been Protestant. Why do you think this is so, and do you foresee changes in the future?

The Role of the Media

In 1868, newspapers and magazines closely followed the dramatic clash between President Andrew Johnson, a Democrat from Tennessee, and the northern Radical Republicans who dominated Congress after the Civil War. President Johnson vetoed their Reconstruction bills and, in defiance of their Tenure of Office Act, fired the secretary of war. Eager to curtail the power of the presidency, the Radicals launched impeachment proceedings, even though it was only months from the end of Johnson's term. On May 16, 1868, the Senate found him "Not guilty" by one vote.

Andrew Johnson's Impeachment Here, the March 21, 1868, issue of *Harper's Weekly* shows Radical Republican Thaddeus Stevens making the closing speech in the House of Representatives.

▲
Improper Influence The press was highly critical of business trusts, which they saw as controlling and corrupting the Presidents of the late nineteenth century. Here President William McKinley (1897-1901) is shown as a child controlled by business trusts while political boss Mark Hanna looks on with approval. McKinley's Vice President, Theodore Roosevelt, is depicted as a child playing soldier on a stick horse.

◄ **Grant Under Fire** The famous newspaper cartoonist Thomas Nast portrayed a beleaguered President Ulysses Grant (1869–1877) shouldering the burdens of corruption and chased by newspapers represented as a pack of dogs.

▲

Roosevelt Projects Confidence As media technology advanced, some Presidents became masters at using it to gain voters' support and exercise influence over other branches of government. One such man was Franklin Delano Roosevelt (1933–1945), shown here delivering a speech that was carried over radio.

Truman Loves the Camera The press corps was out in force to record President Harry Truman (1945–1953) walking to work on the first day of his term. ▶

▲
Richard Nixon accepts the Republican vice presidential nomination.

◀ **"Checkers Speech" Saves Nixon** When Richard Nixon was a vice
presidential candidate (1952), newspapers accused him of profiting from
a political expense fund. He made an emotional presentation on television
to an audience of 58 million (see page 89) and saved his spot on the
ticket. This pro-Nixon cartoon portrays the Democrats (the donkey with
his hand in a jam jar labeled "scandals") as corrupt false accusers.

▲

Ronald Reagan, Mr. Personality A former movie actor, President Reagan was probably the media master of all time. Here he is shown in a motorcade during the inauguration ceremonies in 1981.

◀ **Television and Kennedy** The first ever televised debates between presidential candidates helped John Kennedy narrowly win the 1960 election against Richard Nixon. Although Nixon was more experienced in foreign affairs than Kennedy, he perspired under the camera lights and appeared nervous, while Kennedy was quick, assured, and cool. Later, as President, Kennedy enjoyed televised press conferences, delivering his message with a grace and charm that reminded journalists of the magical kingdom of Camelot.

▲

Carter and the Energy Crisis Concerned about the nation's dependence on imported oil, President Jimmy Carter (1977–1981) asked Americans to make major changes in their lifestyles. Battling special interest groups in the energy and automotive industries, he succeeded with the passage of the National Energy Act.

Reagan and the Air Traffic Controllers' Strike Conservative President Ronald Reagan (1981–1989) took on organized labor when the nation's air traffic controllers struck for higher wages. Insisting that shutting down airports constituted a national emergency, he fired them when they refused to return to work. ▶

▲

Clinton and NAFTA The North American Free Trade Agreement,
or NAFTA, was initiated under President George Bush (1989–1993).
The treaty passed the House in 1993, during the presidency of Bill
Clinton (1993–2001). Here, President Clinton urged its passage,
describing how it would benefit American workers and consumers.

World Leader

chapter 6

Relations with Other Nations

BY PRESIDENT GEORGE WASHINGTON

From the late eighteenth century to the dawn of the twenty-first, the United States has evolved from a loose confederation of insignificant former British colonies to the most powerful country in the world. As the United States has changed, so has the presidency. Nowhere has that change been more dramatic than in the President's role in foreign policy and as a primary leader of the world community.

George Washington, the first President, believed that the new nation was weak and could only be weakened further by becoming involved in European politics and wars. He was not only concerned about British seizure of American merchant vessels, but equally alarmed by the excesses of the French Revolution. In 1796, before he left office, he expressed his non-intervention policy in a farewell address to the nation.

Observe good faith and justice toward all nations. Cultivate peace and harmony with all. Religion and morality **enjoin**[1] this conduct. And can it be that good policy does not equally enjoin it? It will be worthy of a free, enlightened, and, at no distant period, a great nation to give to mankind the **magnanimous**[2] and too novel example of a people always guided by an exalted justice and benevolence. . . .

In the execution of such a plan nothing is more essential than that permanent, **inveterate antipathies**[3] against particular nations and passionate attachments for others should be excluded, and that, in place of them, just and **amicable**[4] feelings toward all should be cultivated. The nation which indulges toward another an habitual hatred or an habitual fondness is in some degree a slave. It is a slave to its animosity or to its affection, either of which is sufficient to lead it astray from its duty and its interest. . . .

The nation prompted by ill will and resentment sometimes impels to war the government, contrary to the best calculations of policy. The government sometimes participates in the national **propensity**[5] and adopts through passion what reason would reject. . . .

So, likewise, a passionate attachment of one nation for another produces a variety of evils. Sympathy for the favorite nation, facilitating the illusion of an imaginary common interest in cases where no real common interest exists, and infusing into one the **enmities**[6] of the other, betrays the former into a participation in the quarrels and wars of the latter without adequate inducement or justification. . . .

---

[1] **enjoin**—command.

[2] **magnanimous**—generous.

[3] **inveterate antipathies**—deep-rooted hostilities.

[4] **amicable**—friendly.

[5] **propensity**—tendency.

[6] **enmities**—hatreds.

As avenues to foreign influence in innumerable ways, such attachments are particularly alarming to the truly enlightened and independent patriot. How many opportunities do they afford to tamper with **domestic factions**,[7] to practice the arts of seduction, to mislead public opinion, to influence or awe the public councils! Such an attachment of a small or weak nation toward a great and powerful nation dooms the former to be the satellite of the latter.

Against the **insidious**[8] wiles of foreign influence (I conjure you to believe me, fellow citizens) the jealousy of a free people ought to be *constantly* awake, since history and experience prove that foreign influence is one of the most baneful foes of republican government. . . .

The great rule of conduct for us in regard to foreign nations is, in extending our commercial relations, to have with them as little *political* connection as possible. So far as we have already formed engagements,[9] let them be fulfilled with perfect good faith. Here let us stop.

Europe has a set of primary interests which to us have none, or a very remote, relation. Hence she must be engaged in frequent controversies, the causes of which are essentially foreign to our concerns. Hence, therefore, it must be unwise in us to implicate ourselves by artificial ties in the ordinary **vicissitudes**[10] of her politics, or the ordinary combinations and collisions of her friendships or enmities.

Our detached and distant situation invites and enables us to pursue a different course. If we remain one people, under an efficient government, the period is not far off when we may defy material injury from external

---

[7] **domestic factions**—opposing groups at home; Washington is referring to emerging political parties and interest groups that foreign countries may side with, increasing tensions within the United States.

[8] **insidious**—deceitful.

[9] Washington is referring to treaties the U.S. signed with France during the Revolutionary War and the Jay Treaty of 1795 with Britain.

[10] **vicissitudes**—difficulties.

annoyance; when we may take such an attitude as will cause the neutrality we may at any time resolve upon to be scrupulously respected; when **belligerent**[11] nations, under the impossibility of making acquisitions upon us, will not lightly hazard the giving us **provocation**;[12] when we may choose peace or war, as our interest, guided by justice, shall counsel.

Why forgo the advantages of so peculiar a situation? Why quit our own to stand upon foreign ground? Why, by interweaving our destiny with that of any part of Europe, entangle our peace and prosperity in the toils of European ambition, rivalship, interest, humor, or caprice?

It is our true policy to steer clear of permanent alliances with any portion of the foreign world, so far, I mean, as we are now at liberty to do it. For let me not be understood as capable of patronizing infidelity to existing engagements.[13] I hold the maxim no less applicable to public than to private affairs that honesty is always the best policy. I repeat, therefore, let those engagements be observed in their genuine sense. But in my opinion it is unnecessary and would be unwise to extend them.

Taking care always to keep ourselves by suitable establishments on a respectable defensive posture, we may safely trust to temporary alliances for extraordinary emergencies.

Harmony, liberal intercourse with all nations, are recommended by policy, humanity, and interest. But even our commercial policy should hold an equal and impartial hand, neither seeking nor granting exclusive favors or preference; . . . constantly keeping in view that it is folly in one nation to look for disinterested favors

---

[11] **belligerent**—warlike.

[12] **provocation**—offense, pushing toward hostilities or war.

[13] patronizing infidelity to existing engagements—dishonoring or ignoring existing agreements.

from another; that it must pay with a portion of its independence for whatever it may accept under that character; that by such acceptance it may place itself in the condition of having given equivalents for nominal favors, and yet of being reproached with ingratitude for not giving more. There can be no greater error than to expect or calculate upon real favors from nation to nation. It is an illusion which experience must cure, which a just pride ought to discard.

QUESTIONS TO CONSIDER

1. What reasons does Washington give for the United States to remain neutral and uninvolved in world politics?

2. How is the role of the United States in world affairs different today from the way it was in Washington's time?

3. Is Washington's advice still appropriate today? Why or why not?

The Monroe Doctrine

BY PRESIDENT JAMES MONROE

The United States was less than fifty years old when President
James Monroe (1817–1825) was faced with two international
situations that threatened American security. First, the Russian tsar,
Alexander, tried to expand his nation's colony in Alaska. Second,
as Spain weakened, more and more of its North and South American
colonies declared independence. Fearing their colonies might revolt
too, the other monarchs of Europe were ready to help the Spanish
recover their colonies and destroy the new Latin American republics.
In response, President Monroe issued a famous warning to European
countries—stay out of the Western Hemisphere. Even though the
United States had almost no international clout in 1823, and
European monarchs were hardly afraid of Monroe, the doctrine
created a foreign policy that allowed the United States to become
a "protector" of the hemisphere.

. . . At the proposal of the Russian Imperial
Government, made through the minister of the Emperor
residing here, a full power and instructions have been

transmitted to the minister of the United States at St. Petersburg[1] to arrange by amicable negotiation the respective rights and interests of the two nations on the northwest coast of this continent. A similar proposal has been made by His Imperial Majesty to the Government of Great Britain, which has likewise been **acceded**[2] to. The Government of the United States has been desirous by this friendly proceeding of manifesting the great value which they have invariably attached to the friendship of the Emperor and their **solicitude**[3] to cultivate the best understanding with his Government. In the discussions to which this interest has given rise and in the arrangements by which they may terminate the occasion has been judged proper for asserting, as a principle in which the rights and interests of the United States are involved, that the American continents, by the free and independent condition which they have assumed and maintain, are henceforth not to be considered as subjects for future colonization by any European powers. . . .

It was stated at the commencement of the last session that a great effort was then being made in Spain and Portugal to improve the condition of the people of those countries, and that it appeared to be conducted with extraordinary moderation. It need scarcely be remarked that the results have been so far very different from what was then anticipated. Of events in that quarter of the globe,[4] with which we have so much **intercourse**[5] and from which we derive our origin, we have always been anxious and interested spectators. The citizens of the United States cherish sentiments the most friendly in favor of the liberty and happiness of their fellow men on that side of the Atlantic. In the wars of the European

---

[1] St. Petersburg—the capital of imperial Russia.

[2] **acceded**—agreed.

[3] **solicitude**—concern.

[4] that quarter of the globe—Europe.

[5] **intercourse**—business; relationship.

powers in matters relating to themselves we have never taken any part, nor does it comport with our policy to do so. It is only when our rights are invaded or seriously **menaced**[6] that we resent injuries or make preparation for our defense. With the movements in this hemisphere we are of necessity more immediately connected, and by causes which must be obvious to all enlightened and impartial observers. The political system of the allied powers[7] is essentially different in this respect from that of America. This difference proceeds from that which exists in their respective Governments; and to the defense of our own, which has been achieved by the loss of so much blood and treasure, and matured by the wisdom of their most enlightened citizens, and under which we have enjoyed **unexampled felicity**,[8] this whole nation is devoted. We owe it, therefore, to candor and to the amicable relations existing between the United States and those powers to declare that we should consider any attempt on their part to extend their system to any portion of this hemisphere as dangerous to our peace and safety. With the existing colonies or dependencies of any European power we have not interfered and shall not interfere. But with the Governments who have declared their independence and maintain it, and whose independence we have, on great consideration and on just principles, acknowledged, we could not view any **interposition**[9] for the purpose of oppressing them, or controlling in any other manner their destiny, by any European power in any other light than as the **manifestation**[10] of an unfriendly disposition toward the United States. In the war between those new Governments and Spain we

---

[6] **menaced**—threatened.

[7] allied powers—Spain and its European allies.

[8] **unexampled felicity**—exceptional happiness.

[9] **interposition**—interference.

[10] **manifestation**—appearance.

declared our neutrality at the time of their recognition, and to this we have adhered, and shall continue to adhere, provided no change shall occur which, in the judgment of the competent authorities of this Government, shall make a corresponding change on the part of the United States indispensable to their security.

The late events in Spain and Portugal show that Europe is still unsettled. Of this important fact no stronger proof can be **adduced**[11] than that the allied powers should have thought it proper, on any principle satisfactory to themselves, to have interposed by force in the internal concerns of Spain. To what extent such interposition may be carried, on the same principle, is a question in which all independent powers whose governments differ from theirs are interested, even those [that are] most remote, and surely none of them more so than the United States. Our policy in regard to Europe, which was adopted at an early stage of the wars which have so long agitated that quarter of the globe, nevertheless remains the same, which is, not to interfere in the internal concerns of any of its powers; to consider the government de facto as the legitimate government for us; to cultivate friendly relations with it, and to preserve those relations by a frank, firm, and manly policy, meeting in all instances the just claims of every power, submitting to injuries from none. But in regard to these continents[12] circumstances are **eminently**[13] and conspicuously different. It is impossible that the allied powers should extend their political system to any portion of either continent without endangering our peace and happiness; nor can anyone believe that our southern brethren,[14] if left to themselves, would adopt it

---

[11] **adduced**—presented.

[12] these continents—North and South America.

[13] **eminently**—greatly.

[14] southern brethren—people of the countries south of the United States, in the Caribbean and Central and South America.

of their own accord. It is equally impossible, therefore, that we should behold such interposition in any form with indifference. If we look to the comparative strength and resources of Spain and those new Governments, and their distance from each other, it must be obvious that she can never subdue them. It is still the true policy of the United States to leave the parties to themselves, in hope that other powers will pursue the same course. . . .

The Monroe Doctrine was expressed during the seventh annual message to Congress, December 2, 1823.

QUESTIONS TO CONSIDER

1. To what international situations is Monroe reacting in his message to Congress?

2. Even though Monroe supports American neutrality in world affairs, how is his foreign policy different from that of President Washington?

3. What influence has the Monroe Doctrine had on American foreign policy? Why is it considered to be a very important document?

Letter to His Son Kermit

BY PRESIDENT THEODORE ROOSEVELT

*Republican Theodore Roosevelt (1901–1909) is widely regarded as
the President who pushed the United States onto the "world stage."
The leader of the Rough Riders unit of the U.S. Army in the
Spanish-American War, Roosevelt supported the U.S. acquisition
of Spanish colonies in Puerto Rico, Guam, and the Philippines.
He approved of America's emergence as a world power and believed
that the U.S. needed a strong navy to protect both its Atlantic
and Pacific coastlines. He fervently backed the U.S. effort to acquire
the rights to build the Panama Canal.*

*As he faced the election of 1904 and his Democratic chal-
lenger Alton Parker, President Roosevelt took time to write this
letter to his fifteen-year-old son, Kermit, who was away at boarding
school. The letter addresses Roosevelt's concerns about the election,
but it also reflects his views on the international responsibilities of
the presidency.*

WHITE HOUSE.
WASHINGTON.

October 26, 1904

Blessed Kermit:

Mother read me your letter in which you want a
"list of the doubtful states," so I am going to write you
a letter about nothing but politics. I enclose you a check
for $5.00 with which you can celebrate after the election
if we win, or console yourself if we lose.

In the first place, be sure not to leave this letter about
where any janitor or anyone else could get a glimpse of
it and make public the information. It wouldn't do to
have our opponents get hold of it, because they would
be sure to twist and garble it.

On the whole this has been an easy campaign for
me, because my real campaign work has been done
during the three years that I have been President; in
other words, I am content to stand or fall on the record
I have made in these three years, and the bulk of
the voters will oppose or support me on that record and
will be only secondarily influenced by what is done during the campaign proper. There remains, however, a
sufficient mass of voters to decide the campaign over-
whelmingly one way or the other, who have to be
aroused from apathy and forced to vote or converted or
kept from going over to the enemy, and it is to influence
these voters that the active management of the
campaign has been directed. In the campaign proper I
made my letter and my speech which have, I think,
formed the basis of our line of attack, and I have taken a
hand in what I regarded as crises, as for instance, in
getting Taft[1] to have Luke Wright cable over denials of

---

[1] Taft—Secretary of Commerce William Howard Taft, a key Roosevelt ally
and, later, his hand-picked successor as President.

Parker's falsehoods about the Philippines. . . . But, speaking generally, I have not had to do much actual work because of the campaign. As you know, while at Oyster Bay,[2] I was really freer and able to enjoy myself more than in previous summers. In a sense, however, this freedom from work has meant more worry, because I have felt as if I was lying still under shell fire just as on the afternoon of the first of July at Santiago.[3] I have continually wished that I could be on the stump myself, and during the last week or ten days I have been fretted at my inability to hit back, and to take the offensive in person against Parker. He lays himself wide open and I could cut him into ribbons if I could get out at him in the open. But of course a President can't go on the stump and can't indulge in personalities, and so I have to sit still and abide the result. I shall be heartily glad when the next two weeks are over and the election is decided one way or the other. I am the first Vice President who became President by the death of his predecessor,[4] who has ever been nominated for the Presidential office. This is no small triumph in itself. As the result of my being President I at least won the unquestioned headship in my own party, and I have to my credit a big sum of substantive achievement—the Panama Canal, the creation of the Department of Commerce and Labor with the Bureau of Corporations, the settlement of the Alaska boundary, the settlement of the Venezuela trouble through the Hague Commission, the success of my policy in Cuba, the success of my policy in the Philippines, the Anthracite Coal Strike, the success of such suits as that against the Northern Securities Company which gave a guaranty in this country that rich man and poor man alike were held equal before the

---

[2] Oyster Bay—the Roosevelt family home on New York's Long Island.

[3] Santiago—site of a key Spanish-American War battle in Cuba.

[4] predecessor—a reference to President William McKinley. Roosevelt was his Vice President and became President when McKinley was assassinated in 1901.

law, and my action in the so-called Miller case which gave to trades-unions a lesson that had been taught corporations—that I favored them while they did right and was not in the least afraid of them when they did wrong.

Now as to the election chances: At present it looks as if the odds were in my favor, but I have no idea whether this appearance is deceptive or not. I am a very positive man and Parker is a very negative man, and in consequence I both attract supporters and make enemies that he does not, in a way that he cannot. He can be painted any color to please any audience; but it is impossible to make two different pictures of any side of my character. I have done a great many things and said a great many things, and a great many people who like my general course dislike some particular thing I have said or done. Often people are against me for directly conflicting reasons. Thus, the *Evening Post* and Carl Schurz profess loud sympathy for my attitude toward the colored man of the South, but in spite of this oppose me because of my attitude toward the Filipinos. On the other hand, *Collier's Weekly* and a much larger body of men profess great sympathy with my attitude toward the Filipinos, but attack me because of my attitude toward the colored man of the South. These two sets of people are therefore diametrically opposed to one another, and for diametrically opposite reasons unite in the one point of opposing me. As a matter of fact I am right both as regards the point upon which the *Evening Post* attacks me and as regards the point upon which *Collier's Weekly* attacks me! but the fact that I am right does not alter the further fact that because of my attitude on both points I lose a certain number of votes. In the same way the great capitalists who object to any restraint being exercised over the deeds of corporations oppose me, while the rather hysterical men who want to go to lengths against capital, and especially against corporate wealth, which would bring ruin to this country, also oppose me. So it is in many other matters.

There are thus many conflicting currents of feeling. I will have accessions of strength of unknown force, and I have repelled interests whose actual effect on election day we cannot now reckon. It is, therefore, utterly impossible to say what the outcome will be. The betting is in my favor, and our people are very confident that I will be elected. Some of our opponents are not so confident in Parker's success, but those at headquarters undoubtedly are. Moreover, in the next ten days there is always the possibility that something will happen that will upset all calculations. So what I am about to say you must remember is a guess only and I may be hopelessly wrong at that, but you shall have my guess in detail as to actual conditions.

We need 239 votes in the electoral college to give me a majority. Of these I think we are practically sure to have 200 from the following states: California 10, Illinois 27, Iowa 13, Kansas 10, Maine 6, Massachusetts 16, Michigan 14, Minnesota 11, Nebraska 8, New Hampshire 4, North Dakota 4, Ohio 23, Oregon 4, Pennsylvania 34, South Dakota 4, Vermont 4, Washington 5, Wyoming 3. Then in addition it looks now as though we should probably carry the states of Wisconsin 13, Utah 3, Connecticut 7, New Jersey 12, Idaho 3, which number 38 votes all told. This leaves us just one short of a majority, and we now come into the region of entire doubt. I should put the following states as doubtful: New York 39, Rhode Island 4, Delaware 3, Indiana 15, West Virginia 7, Colorado 5, Montana 3, Nevada 3, 79 votes. If we get all those I have enumerated as sure and as probably our way, and also any one of these doubtful states, we win. Then, in addition, there is a very small chance of carrying Nevada or Maryland, and an even smaller chance of carrying Missouri; but in all probability these three states will vote in company with the eleven ex-

Confederate states, which are solidly Democratic, because there is in reality no popular election in them and their Democratic majorities represent a mixture of force and fraud.[5]

From the above you will see how difficult it is to make anything like a certain guess. In New York the revolt against what people call, without exactly understanding it, Odellism[6] threatens defeat to the State ticket, although our nominee, Higgins, is a most admirable man. If it were not for this revolt I am very sure I should carry New York by a large majority, but it is perfectly possible that the revolt may bring me down in ruin as well as Higgins, although I hope the contrary will take place and that instead of the State ticket pulling me down to defeat I shall pull through the State ticket to victory. Indiana ought to go our way, but Bryan[7] has made a most telling canvass there for Parker, while Cleveland[8] has helped Parker in the East. You see the Democratic canvass is absolutely double-faced. In the East they are trying to get everybody to vote for them on the ground that if Parker and his people keep control of the Democratic organization it means the death of Bryanism. In the West they try to get votes by saying that the success of Parker really means the success of Bryanism and Bryan's ultimate mastery of the party which will control the country.

So, Kermit, we shall know nothing about the result until the votes are counted, and in the meanwhile must possess our souls in patience. If things go wrong remember that we are very, very fortunate to have had

---

[5] Roosevelt actually won the election with 336 electoral votes to Parker's 140, and 7,628,461 popular votes to Parker's 5,084,223.

[6] Odellism—The conservative policies of Republican Benjamin Odell, who succeeded Roosevelt as governor of New York in 1901.

[7] Bryan—William Jennings Bryan, the unsuccessful Democratic nominee for President in 1896, 1900, and 1908.

[8] Cleveland—former Democratic President Grover Cleveland (1885–1889 and 1893–1897).

three years in the White House, and that I have had a chance to accomplish work such as comes to very, very few men in any generation; and that I have no business to feel downcast or **querulous**[9] merely because when so much has been given me I have not had even more.

Your loving father,
Theodore Roosevelt

---

[9] **querulous**—inclined to blame others; dissatisfied.

QUESTIONS TO CONSIDER

1. In weighing his chances in the 1904 presidential election, what does Theodore Roosevelt see as his strengths and weaknesses?

2. Based on Roosevelt's description, what differences do you see in elections then and now? What similarities?

3. What evidence does this letter contain that the President in 1904 had many more international responsibilities than those a century before?

"A Date Which Will Live in Infamy"

BY PRESIDENT FRANKLIN ROOSEVELT

*The United States had reluctantly joined the Allies in World War I.
After the war, the Republican Presidents of the 1920s—Warren
Harding, Calvin Coolidge and Herbert Hoover—favored a return to
isolationism. The economic problems of the 1930s kept Democratic
President Franklin D. Roosevelt (1933–1945) focused on domestic
concerns. When Hitler began conquering all of Europe, the United
States was not eager to get involved. Only after the Japanese
attacked Pearl Harbor, the Hawaiian headquarters of the U.S. Navy's
Pacific fleet, was the nation unquestioningly involved. In this famous
address to Congress, broadcast live on national radio, Roosevelt
asked for a declaration of war against Japan. He went on to play
a major role in the leadership of the Allied forces of World War II
and in the planning for new world relationships that would come
after it was over.*

TO THE CONGRESS OF THE UNITED STATES:

Yesterday, December 7, 1941—a date which will live in **infamy**[1]—the United States of America was suddenly and deliberately attacked by naval and air forces of the Empire of Japan.

The United States was at peace with that Nation and, at the **solicitation**[2] of Japan, was still in conversation with its Government and its Emperor, looking toward the maintenance of peace in the Pacific. Indeed, one hour after Japanese air squadrons had commenced bombing in Oahu, the Japanese Ambassador to the United States and his colleague delivered to the Secretary of State a form reply to a recent American message. While this reply stated that it seemed useless to continue the existing diplomatic negotiations, it contained no threat or hint of war or armed attack.

It will be recorded that the distance of Hawaii from Japan makes it obvious that the attack was deliberately planned many days or even weeks ago. During the intervening time the Japanese Government had deliberately sought to deceive the United States by false statements and expressions of hope for continued peace.

The attack yesterday on the Hawaiian Islands has caused severe damage to American naval and military forces. Very many American lives have been lost. In addition American ships have been reported torpedoed on the high seas between San Francisco and Honolulu.

Yesterday the Japanese Government also launched an attack against Malaya.

Last night Japanese forces attacked Hong Kong.

Last night Japanese forces attacked Guam.

Last night Japanese forces attacked the Philippine Islands.

---

[1] **infamy**—shame.

[2] **solicitation**—earnest request.

Last night the Japanese attacked Midway Island.

Japan has, therefore, undertaken a surprise offensive extending throughout the Pacific area. The facts of yesterday speak for themselves. The people of the United States have already formed their opinions and well understand the implications to the very life and safety of our Nation.

As Commander-in-Chief of the Army and Navy I have directed that all measures be taken for our defense.

Always will we remember the character of the onslaught against us.

No matter how long it may take us to overcome this **premeditated**[3] invasion, the American people in their righteous might will win through to absolute victory.

I believe I interpret the will of the Congress and of the people when I assert that we will not only defend ourselves to the uttermost but will make very certain that this form of treachery shall never endanger us again.

Hostilities exist. There is no blinking at the fact that our people, our territory, and our interests are in grave danger.

With confidence in our armed forces—with the unbounded determination of our people—we will gain the inevitable triumph—so help us God.

I ask that the Congress declare that since the unprovoked and **dastardly**[4] attack by Japan on Sunday, December seventh, a state of war has existed between the United States and the Japanese Empire.

Franklin D. Roosevelt
The White House, December 8, 1941

---

[3] **premeditated**—planned in advance.
[4] **dastardly**—sneaky, malicious, and cowardly.

QUESTIONS TO CONSIDER

1. What Japanese actions other than the bombing of Pearl Harbor does Roosevelt cite to justify the United States' declaration of war?

2. Why is Roosevelt's address directed to Congress?

3. What role does the President play in wartime?

from   .

Eisenhower and the Cold War

BY ROBERT A. DIVINE

*With the conclusion of World War II, the United States emerged
as a "superpower," forever turning its back on isolationism. World
War II hero General Dwight Eisenhower became President in 1953
during the height of Cold War tensions with the Soviet Union. A
widely accepted perception of Eisenhower's presidency (1953–1961)
was that the Republican was popular and grandfatherly, but had
neither the desire nor the talent to forge an assertive foreign policy
for the country. Eisenhower, according to this view, left foreign affairs
to Secretary of State John Foster Dulles while he played golf and
made speeches. However, historian Robert A. Divine finds Eisenhower
to be a much more complex President, one who was fully capable
of creating, controlling, and implementing an effective Cold War
foreign policy.*

World War II would serve ever after as Eisenhower's
point of reference on world affairs. In common with
others of his generation, he viewed appeasement and

the Munich Conference[1] as the **epitome**[2] of diplomatic folly. Isolationism was just as bad; "no intelligent man can be an isolationist," he commented to the people of Abilene, Kansas, in June 1945. The United States must remain active in the world, assuming its rightful role of leadership. Despite his service in the Philippines, he was European-centered in his thinking. He shared the Eastern establishment's foreign policy view that American security rested on a stable and friendly Europe, and he had little patience for those Republicans who were oriented toward Asia. Above all, he saw himself as a champion of peace, the soldier who would cap his service to the nation by working for international harmony. Yet even here he had little patience for those who spoke of an ideal world without conflict. Peace, to Eisenhower, was a practical matter. Nations would always have competing interests; the real task was to avoid the resort to armed force. "We must learn in this world," he told John Gunther [a journalist] in 1951, "to accommodate ourselves so that we may live at peace with others whose basic philosophy may be very different."

Eisenhower's outlook on the world grew directly from his personality. Just as he believed that common sense and good will could resolve almost any problem between individuals, he felt that nations could exist in harmony despite their differences. Throughout his career, he had displayed, as Gunther noted, an "instinctive ability to understand the other person's point of view." This **empathy**,[3] combined with a buoyant optimism, set him at odds with Cold Warriors who believed that the United States was locked in a struggle for

---

[1] At the Munich Conference in 1938, British Prime Minister Neville Chamberlain, believing he could keep peace by giving in to Hitler's demands, persuaded his allies in France to honor Hitler's claim to the Sudetenland in exchange for a promise to stay out of the rest of Czechoslovakia.

[2] **epitome**—prime example.

[3] **empathy**—compassion.

survival with the Soviet Union. The clash with the Russians, which he inherited from Truman, was a problem to be managed, not an all-consuming crusade against the forces of evil.... He had the ability to stand aloof from the passions of the moment and to assess the broader implications of each situation. . . . What some perceived as excessive caution and even indecision would prove in time to be admirable qualities of patience and prudence that enabled Eisenhower to deal effectively with many of the international crises of the 1950s.

The Cold War was at its height in the spring of 1952 when Dwight Eisenhower decided to seek the Republican nomination. The Marshall Plan had helped to put Europe back on its feet economically, but the process of creating an effective NATO[4] defense force had barely gotten started under Eisenhower. There were only a dozen NATO divisions to counter the more than one hundred Soviet formations, and the problem of German rearmament still divided the Western allies. In Asia, the Korean War had settled into a stalemate after the Chinese intervention in late 1950; truce talks that had begun in mid-1951 were stalled over the delicate issue of repatriating unwilling prisoners-of-war. The most **ominous**[5] development came in the nuclear field, where the Soviets had broken the American atomic monopoly by detonating their first bomb in August 1949. The United States had responded with a crash program to perfect the far more awesome hydrogen bomb, and after a crucial theoretical breakthrough in the spring of 1951, the American H-bomb program was in high gear, with the first test explosion set for the fall of

---

[4] NATO—the North Atlantic Treaty Organization. This post-World War II military alliance of the United States, Canada and their European allies, was established to defend Western Europe against possible Soviet aggression. Eisenhower was its first commander.

[5] **ominous**—threatening.

1952. And the Soviets were only a few months behind in their secret quest for the H-bomb.

Foreign policy posed a difficult political problem for the Republican party. In both the 1944 and 1948 elections, the GOP had chosen not to challenge the Democrats on international affairs, opting instead for a bipartisan position. John Foster Dulles, an experienced international lawyer and diplomat, had advised defeated candidate Thomas Dewey to pursue such a policy, but by the spring of 1952 Dulles had changed his mind. He felt it was vital for the Republicans to challenge the Democratic policy of containment[6] and to promise the American people a new and bolder stance in world affairs.

In early May, Dulles flew to Paris to confer with Dwight Eisenhower at his NATO headquarters. He brought with him an essay he had written on American foreign policy which would be published three weeks later in *Life* magazine. Warning that containment would lead ultimately to both excessive reliance on military power and to a heavy drain on the American economy, Dulles outlined two new approaches. The first he called **retaliation**.[7] Instead of investing so heavily in conventional military power to contain the threat of Communist aggression, Dulles suggested a reliance on America's air and nuclear superiority. Without ever mentioning the atomic bomb, he hinted at a willingness to use it as a threat against the Soviet Union. "The free world," he argued, should "develop the will and organize the means to retaliate instantly against open aggression by Red armies, so that, if it occurred anywhere, we could and would strike back where it hurts, by means of our own choosing."

---

[6] containment—a foreign policy followed by the U.S. government under President Truman. Its goal was to "contain" Communism, or keep it from spreading to any new areas of the world.

[7] **retaliation**—revenge; punishment.

The use of nuclear weapons to neutralize Soviet conventional superiority would enable the United States to implement a new political strategy of liberation. Bemoaning the postwar Russian domination of Eastern Europe, Dulles advocated a moral and spiritual offensive to free these captive nations. The United States should abandon the static policy of containment and instead make it "publicly known that it wants and expects liberation to occur." He did not, however, advocate the use of force. He spoke vaguely about using Radio Free Europe to encourage people to escape from behind the Iron Curtain,[8] and the organization of "task forces" to develop "freedom programs" for each of the captive nations. It might take a decade or more for liberation to occur, but he was confident that in the long run the forces of freedom and democracy would triumph over those of oppression and tyranny.

Eisenhower, who had read earlier drafts of Dulles's essay, was impressed by the concepts of retaliation and liberation. They fitted in with his belief that containment could lead to eventual American bankruptcy. He made no comment about liberation, but he challenged the simplistic notion that all Communist moves could be met with the threat of nuclear war. He wondered how retaliation could be used to counter "Soviet political aggression, as in Czechoslovakia," which "successively chips away exposed portions of the free world." From his experience with NATO, Eisenhower realized the importance of conventional forces[9] "to convey a feeling of confidence to exposed populations, a confidence which will make them sturdier, politically, in their opposition to Communist inroads."

---

[8] Iron Curtain—a phrase coined by Winston Churchill to describe the imaginary barrier that separated the Soviet Union and its Communist satellites from the non-Communist world.

[9] conventional forces—traditional, non-nuclear warfare.

After their meeting in France, Dulles agreed to support Eisenhower's candidacy, but he withheld any public announcement while he strove to hammer out a Republican foreign-policy plank acceptable to both the general and to his main opponent, Senator Robert Taft. The document that finally emerged, after considerable amendment by Taft's supporters, was highly **partisan**[10] in tone. The Republicans accused the Democrats of abandoning the peoples of Eastern Europe to Communist rule in the "tragic blunders" made at Teheran, Yalta, and Potsdam.[11] A specific repudiation of the Yalta agreement was coupled with a ringing call for the liberation of "captive peoples." Instead of continuing "the negative, **futile**[12] and immoral policy of 'containment,'" the GOP platform promised to "revive the contagious, liberating influences which are inherent in freedom." Eisenhower accepted this partisan rhetoric, presumably as the price he had to pay for party unity, but he drew the line at the inclusion of the phrase "retaliatory striking power" in the platform. The general felt this meant exclusive reliance on air power and the abandonment of all that he had done to build up NATO. . . .

After winning the Republican nomination, Eisenhower seemed willing to embrace the second Dulles slogan, "liberation," in the fall campaign. The promise to take the offensive in the Cold War had great domestic political appeal, especially to ethnic groups such as Polish Americans who normally voted Democratic. Thus in his first major foreign-policy speech, given at the American Legion convention in late August, Eisenhower declared his opposition to the Soviet tyranny, "a tyranny that has brought thousands,

---

[10] **partisan**—favoring one political party over the other.

[11] Teheran, Yalta, and Potsdam—the conferences of the United States, Britain, and the Soviet Union during World War II in which the future of postwar Europe was determined.

[12] **futile**—useless.

millions of people into slave camps and is attempting to make all humankind its **chattel**."[13] Without specifying how it would be done, he called upon the American people to join with him in a great moral crusade to liberate the captive peoples. . . . The next day, after a long conference with the candidate, Dulles reaffirmed the liberation concept, telling reporters that what the United States needed to do was to "try to split the satellite states away" from Russia. "The only way to stop a head-on collision with the Soviet Union is to break it up from within," Dulles concluded.

The Republican liberation rhetoric sent a shudder through Western Europe. Frightened by the prospect of a nuclear war to free the captive nations, Europeans wondered what had happened to the **prudent**[14] Eisenhower they had known and trusted. At home, the Democrats made the most of their opportunity. Candidate Adlai Stevenson spoke sadly about the risk of a war which would "liberate only broken, silent and empty lands.". . .

Eisenhower himself was disturbed by the implications of liberation. Upset that Dulles had failed to stress the vital qualification that liberation should be achieved only by peaceful means, the candidate berated him for this omission after a speech in Buffalo in which Dulles talked about air-drops of supplies to anti-Communist freedom fighters. In his next major foreign policy address, the general restated the liberation concept in carefully qualified terms, saying that he intended "to aid by every peaceful means, but only by peaceful means, the right to live in freedom." Then he stressed his devotion to peace by concluding, "The one—the only—way to win World War III is to prevent it."

---

[13] **chattel**—property.
[14] **prudent**—sensible.

This speech in Philadelphia on September 4 marks the end of Eisenhower's reliance on liberation in the campaign. He dropped all further references to captive peoples, save for one brief Pulaski Day statement, and he no longer relied on Dulles for drafts of foreign policy speeches. For Eisenhower, the political advantages in liberation were more than outweighed by the implication that he favored a policy that could lead to war with the Soviet Union. His own devotion to peace prevailed.

Eisenhower's handling of the Korean War issue showed that he was still willing to exploit foreign policy for political gain. When the war first broke out in June 1950, he staunchly backed Truman's decision to fight, and he stood behind the President when he removed General MacArthur.[15] The stalemate in Korea had made the war increasingly unpopular by 1952, and even though other Republicans sniped at Truman's policy, Eisenhower remained loyal. In his first press conference after declaring his candidacy in June, the general expressed his doubts about launching a major offensive in Korea to achieve victory and then added, "I do not believe that in the present situation there is any clean-cut answer to bringing the Korean War to a successful conclusion."

By the fall, Eisenhower felt differently. Surveys of public opinion and voter sentiment revealed a growing national concern with the stalemated conflict and a belief that Eisenhower could furnish the new leadership needed to end the fighting. The candidate began making references to the war in Korea, defending Truman's decision to fight but questioning his conduct of the war. In early October, he took a new line by suggesting that the [Truman] administration was wrong in making American youth bear the brunt of battle. "That is a job

---

[15] General MacArthur—Douglas MacArthur, a famous general in charge of United Nations troops in Korea, was dismissed by President Truman for his aggressive war tactics and refusal to obey the President's directions.

for Koreans," he said in Illinois. "If there must be a war there, let it be Asians against Asians, with our support on the side of freedom." A few days later in San Francisco, Ike stressed the heavy casualties the United States had suffered in Korea and then for the first time stated that if elected he would give "full dedication to the job of finding an intelligent and honorable way to end the tragic toll. . . ."

Even as Eisenhower was speaking, the dormant war sprang to life. The Communists broke the lull with a major offensive on October 6; a week later, General Mark Clark ordered a counter-strike. For two weeks, American troops, engaged in bitter, hand-to-hand fighting in the "Iron Triangle" area, suffered heavy casualties. The Democrats, on the defensive, accused the Republican candidate of trying to wring votes out of "our ugly, miserable, bloody ordeal" in Korea. President Truman, angry at Eisenhower's **intimation**[16] that he knew how to end the conflict, dared Ike to come forward with his remedy.

Truman's challenge played directly into the hands of the Republican strategists. Several of Eisenhower's advisers, including speechwriter Emmet Hughes, thought that Korea was a perfect issue on which to apply the general's reputation as a military expert. Hughes wrote a speech in which the candidate would promise to go to Korea if he were elected. He gave it to campaign manager Sherman Adams, who immediately approved, but they were afraid that Ike would reject it as too theatrical. When they showed the text to the general, however, his eyes lit up, he reached for a pencil, and quickly made a few changes to sharpen the impact of the key sentence.

Eisenhower made his famous pledge at the height of the campaign, in a speech in Detroit on October 24. He

---

[16] **intimation**—hint.

singled out Korea as the tragedy that "challenges all men dedicated to the work of peace." After accusing the Democrats of mishandling the war, he came to his climax. The first task of a new administration, he declared, would be "to bring the Korean war to an early and honorable end." "That job requires a personal trip to Korea," he continued. "I shall make that trip. . . . I shall go to Korea."

"That does it—Ike is in," reporters told Sherman Adams. Nearly all the political commentators agreed that the pledge to go to Korea clinched the election for Eisenhower. He repeated the promise in subsequent speeches, driving home the belief in the minds of voters that the architect of victory in World War II would surely find a way to conclude the limited war in Asia. The beauty of the pledge, however, lay in its very vagueness. All that Eisenhower promised was to make the trip. He left himself complete freedom of action in dealing with the Korean conflict as President. He had thus been able to take political advantage of the Korean War without committing himself in advance to any specific course of action.

After Eisenhower's decisive victory at the polls over Adlai Stevenson, most observers assumed that one of his first acts as President-elect would be to appoint John Foster Dulles as secretary of state. Instead, Ike delayed the appointment for several weeks while he canvassed the field. For a time he considered offering the position to John J. McCloy, a leading member of the foreign policy establishment and former American High Commissioner to Germany. Eisenhower finally settled on Dulles, partly out of his respect for his knowledge and experience in foreign policy and partly because Ike knew that the appointment would please the Taft wing of the GOP.

In the course of time, the legend grew that Eisenhower turned over foreign policy completely to his secretary of state, intervening only occasionally to soften the unyielding line that Dulles pursued toward the Soviet Union. . . .

There is much in the relationship of the two men, however, which does not fit this simple picture. From the outset, Dulles was insecure in his relations with Eisenhower. The President kept him dangling before he appointed him secretary of state, and throughout his presidency, Eisenhower kept a set of independent foreign-policy advisers on hand at the White House. Dulles constantly struggled to prevent men like C. D. Jackson, Nelson Rockefeller, and Harold Stassen from using their White House posts to influence the course of American foreign policy. Adams tells of the frequency of Dulles's visits to the President's office and of the constant telephone calls from the secretary of state, a fact confirmed by the logs kept by the White House staff. In his own memoirs, Ike refers casually to the fact that while traveling abroad, "Secretary Dulles made a constant practice . . . of cabling me a summary of the day's events." After six years, Ike recalled, the cables and other memoranda from Dulles made a stack more than four feet high—hardly an indication of a secretary of state making policy on his own.

In essence, Eisenhower used Dulles. Confident of his own grasp of world affairs, he needed someone who had the knowledge and skill to conduct diplomacy yet would defer to the President. Ike also realized the importance of having a secretary of state who could keep **ardent**[17] Cold Warriors, especially right-wing Republican senators, happy with administration policy. He knew how helpless Dean Acheson[18] had become, called constantly to testify before congressional committees to justify Truman's policies, which were in fact

[17] **ardent**—zealous, intense.
[18] Dean Acheson—Secretary of State under President Truman.

tough and unyielding toward the Soviet Union. Dulles could serve as the lightning rod, absorbing domestic criticism and warding off attacks from the right with his moralistic rhetoric. On occasion, Ike would complain that "Foster is just too worried about being accused of sounding like Truman and Acheson," but he understood the advantage of having the secretary of state as the target of criticism. "The Democrats love to hit him rather than me," Ike commented to Emmet Hughes. And Ike never had any doubts about who called the shots. ". . . there's only one man I know who has seen *more* of the world and talked with more people and *knows* more than he does," Eisenhower told Hughes, "—and that's me."

The two men formed an effective team. Eisenhower enjoyed the confidence of the American people, and he had a personal relationship with many of the world's leaders. Pragmatic by nature, he was committed to an effort to keep the Cold War manageable, to reduce tensions, and to avoid the dread possibility of a nuclear war. Dulles had a more theoretical cast of mind. Convinced of America's moral superiority, he sought to put the Communists on the defensive. His moralistic and often ponderous public statements gave him the reputation, which he cherished, of being a dedicated crusader against the Soviets; behind the scenes, he proved to have a lucid understanding of the realities of world politics and a surprising gift for the give-and-take of diplomacy. Dulles, the civilian lawyer, had a fondness for the threat of force, while Eisenhower, the military man, preferred the language of peaceful persuasion. The secretary tended to become uneasy in moments of crisis; the President was at his best when the situation became the most tense. One close associate commented about Eisenhower's air of calm relaxation during a critical period: "I realized as never before why a President is so important—to be able to give others, at such a time, an impression of unruffled assurance and confidence.". . .

Above all, the two men complemented each other. Ike lacked the stamina and enthusiasm for the daily grind of diplomacy that Dulles took in stride. Though the President was knowledgeable about European issues, he was much weaker on Asia, Latin America, and the Middle East. Dulles helped fill in many of the gaps in Eisenhower's understanding of world affairs. Eisenhower's serene self-confidence helped offset Dulles's personal insecurity. When the secretary fretted about public opinion and the reactions of others, the President could offer him the necessary reassurance, telling him to ignore his critics. And there was no doubt in either man's mind who made the decisions that counted. "The truth is that Dulles did Eisenhower's bidding in matters of high policy," comments presidential biographer Peter Lyon, "and also served as the convenient butt for any criticism of that policy. . . ." Ann Whitman, Eisenhower's private secretary, wrote to a friend after Dulles's death to play down reports of a "new" Eisenhower finally taking command of American foreign policy. "He isn't any different—he has always taken the lead," she wrote. "Perhaps now it is more obvious, but Dulles and the President consulted on every decision and then Dulles went back to the State Department and carried them out."

QUESTIONS TO CONSIDER

1. What, according to Divine, was Eisenhower's view of international relations?

2. What were the issues in foreign affairs that the Republican platform, drafted by Dulles, addressed?

3. In what ways did Eisenhower differ from Dulles?

4. How did Eisenhower take political advantage of the Korean War?

5. How did Eisenhower use his Secretary of State in the formation and execution of foreign policy? Give examples.

Johnson and the Vietnam War

BY DORIS KEARNS GOODWIN

By the mid-1960s Cold War politics focused on American involvement in Vietnam. American foreign policy was built on the idea of "containment," the belief that the most important American objective should be to contain Communism and keep it from spreading into new areas. After China became Communist in 1949, that movement threatened to spread to other areas of Asia. Americans feared the "domino theory," which held that if one Southeast Asian country fell to Communism, all of them would follow like a row of dominoes collapsing on each other. Lyndon Johnson, President from 1963 to 1969, faced difficult, controversial decisions regarding the American commitment to fight Communism in South Vietnam. This war eventually ended in humiliation and defeat for the United States in 1975. In the following excerpt, historian and television commentator Doris Kearns Goodwin explains how some of those fateful decisions were made.

Without personal contact, Johnson tended to see foreign leaders as remote, **uncanny**[1] figures and was uncomfortable with their strangeness. During three decades at the seat of the government, he had learned the accepted concepts of international conflict, containment, **bipolarity**,[2] limited war. But he didn't think in that language. He thought in terms of personalities, power, and good works.

South Vietnam was ten thousand miles away. Johnson had visited it once, for three days. He had then met Ngo Dinh Diem,[3] but now Diem was dead and he knew almost nothing about his successor. Skeptical of his own ability to sort out the complicated strands of religion, party, and culture, Johnson turned to others for guidance, in particular to John Kennedy's men:[4] Robert McNamara, McGeorge Bundy, Dean Rusk, and Maxwell Taylor. All these men had previously committed themselves to the maintenance of an independent non-Communist South Vietnam. All of them shared the view that Vietnam was a critical testing ground of America's ability to counter Communist support for wars of national liberation.[5] Moreover, they reflected the generally held position of the foreign policy establishment that had dominated America's conduct of foreign affairs since the cold war began.

That Johnson was strongly influenced by these advisers is clear; they were Kennedy's men and they had expertise in the one area he knew the least about. But he was not, as some have pictured, a passive figure,

---

[1] **uncanny**—mysterious.

[2] **bipolarity**—a world controlled by two strong, opposite powers; meaning the United States and the Soviet Union.

[3] Ngo Dinh Diem—South Vietnam's president in the early 1960s.

[4] John Kennedy's men—Johnson became President when John Kennedy was assassinated. While he was completing Kennedy's term of office, Johnson kept most of Kennedy's advisers and cabinet members in place.

[5] wars of national liberation—wars in which Communist rebels were trying to overthrow pro-U.S. governments.

a **dupe**[6] to their advice. He accepted their advice to continue the policy of supporting South Vietnam because it accorded with a set of assumptions he had long held about the nature of Communism and the importance of Southeast Asia. These assumptions are delineated in this conversation with [Democratic Senator] William Fulbright[7] on March 2, 1964:

PRESIDENT: If we can just get our foreign policy straightened out.

FULBRIGHT: Get that . . . Vietnam straightened out. Any hope?

PRESIDENT: Well, we've got about four possibilities. The only thing I know to do is more of the same and do it more efficiently and effectively and we got a problem out there that I inherited with Lodge.[8] I wire him every day and say what else do you recommend? Here is the best summary we have. (1) In Southeast Asia the free world is facing an attempt by the Communists of North Vietnam to subvert and overthrow the non-Communist government of South Vietnam. North Vietnam has been providing direction, control, and training for 25,000 Vietcong[9] guerrillas. (2) Our objective, our purpose in South Vietnam, is to help the Vietnamese maintain their independence. We are providing the training and logistic support they cannot provide themselves. We will continue to provide that support as long as it is required. As soon as the mission is complete our troops can be withdrawn. There's no reason to keep our military police there when the Vietnamese are

---

[6] **dupe**—easily tricked person.

[7] William Fulbright—Senator from Arkansas; Chairman of the Foreign Relations Committee.

[8] Lodge—U.S. Ambassador to South Vietnam Henry Cabot Lodge.

[9] Vietcong—Communist rebels in South Vietnam who supported the North Vietnamese.

trained for that purpose. (3) In the past four months there've been three governments in South Vietnam. The Vietcong have taken advantage of this confusion. Their increased activity has had success. At least four alternatives are open to us: (1) Withdraw from South Vietnam. Without our support the government will be unable to counter the aid from the North to the Vietcong. Vietnam will collapse and the ripple effect will be felt throughout Southeast Asia, endangering independent governments in Thailand, Malaysia, and extending as far as India and Indonesia and the Philippines. (2) We can seek a formula that will neutralize South Vietnam à la Mansfield and De Gaulle[10] but any such formula will only lead in the end to the same results as withdrawing support. We all know the Communist attitude that what's mine is mine, what's yours is negotiable. True neutralization would have to extend to North Vietnam and this has been specifically rejected by North Vietnam and the Communist China government, and we believe if we attempted to neutralize, the Commies would stay in North Vietnam. We would abandon South Vietnam. The Communists would take over South Vietnam. (3) We can send Marines à la Goldwater[11] and other U.S. forces against the sources of these aggressions but our men may well be bogged down in a long war against numerically superior North Vietnamese and Chicom[12] forces 100,000 miles from home. (4) We [can] continue our present policy of providing training and logistical support of South Vietnamese forces. This policy has not failed. We

---

[10] Senator Mike Mansfield and French President Charles De Gaulle supported making South Vietnam a neutral nation unallied with the West or the Communists.

[11] Goldwater—Senator Barry Goldwater, who would become the Republican nominee for President against Johnson in the 1964 election.

[12] Chicom—Chinese Communist.

propose to continue it. [Defense] Secretary McNamara's trip to South Vietnam will provide us with an opportunity to again appraise the prospects of the policy and the future alternatives open to us.

FULBRIGHT: I think that's right . . . that's exactly what I'd arrive at under these circumstances at least for the foreseeable future.

PRESIDENT: Now when he [McNamara] comes back though and if we're losing with what we're doing, we've got to decide whether to send them in or whether to come out and let the dominoes fall. That's where the tough one is going to be. And you do some heavy thinking and let's decide what we do.

FULBRIGHT: Righto.

Although Johnson shared the general outlook of his advisers, he was far from deciding what means should be employed—whether, indeed, the objectives were possible of fulfillment. He had, after all, not approved an earlier proposal to use American military force to prevent Ho Chi Minh's victory over the French.[13] He did know that these were difficult decisions to be made. But he needed time, and in any event an election year was no time to make them. The word went out that tough decisions on Vietnam should be deferred as long as possible. The glimpses of the President revealed in *The Pentagon Papers*[14] show a man determined to achieve the goal of an independent non-Communist South Vietnam, yet holding back on actions to achieve that goal until he believed they were desperately, absolutely necessary.

---

[13] Ho Chi Minh's victory over the French—Vietnam, both North and South, was controlled by the French until 1954, when the Vietnamese Communist leader defeated them at the battle of Dien Bien Phu. This led to the division of the country into a Communist North and a pro-U.S. South.

[14] *The Pentagon Papers*—secret intelligence reports given by a State Department employee to *The New York Times* for publication in 1971.

In the spring of 1964, opinion surveys showed that more than two-thirds of the American public said they paid little or no attention to what was going on in Vietnam. Johnson wanted to keep it that way. Rejecting proposals to expand the war into North Vietnam, or to introduce combat troops in the South, Johnson believed that he was, for now, left with only one choice: **incremental**[15] and **covert**[16] escalation of military pressure, designed to convince Hanoi[17] that the United States was serious and to reassure Saigon.[18] Nonetheless, in the next few months, the situation in South Vietnam continued to deteriorate and the Saigon regime was shaken by one crisis after another. Yet the established official consensus on Vietnam and its significance held firm.

The only time his will seemed fully engaged in Vietnam policy came in August when an American destroyer was supposedly attacked by the North Vietnamese. He saw it as an opportunity to show the seriousness of our commitment to South Vietnam. Within twelve hours after news of the incident reached Washington, American bombers were dispatched on a reprisal raid over North Vietnam. Two days later, the administration asked the Congress "to approve and support the determination of the President as Commander in Chief to take all the necessary measures to repel any armed attack against the forces of the United States to prevent further aggression.... The United States regards Vietnam as vital to its national interest and to world peace and security in Southeast Asia."

William Fulbright guided the Tonkin Gulf Resolution[19] through the Senate, with only Wayne

---

[15] **incremental**—increasing.

[16] **covert**—secret.

[17] Hanoi—the capital of Communist North Vietnam.

[18] Saigon—the capital of U.S.-supported South Vietnam.

[19] Tonkin Gulf Resolution—a resolution giving the President broad powers to wage war in Vietnam. The resolution was Congress's response to two apparent attacks on the destroyer *Maddox* in the Gulf of Tonkin.

Morse and Ernest Gruening in dissent. In the House, the vote was unanimous, 416 to 0. Congress had, without knowing, established the formal foundation that would later be used to support a full-scale war.

In one stroke, Johnson had been able both to flex his muscles and to show restraint, to act abroad as he had done at home with the tax cut and the poverty program: pursue contradictory policies and apparently make them work. Running as the "man of peace," the man who would "never send American boys to do the fighting that Asian boys should do themselves," Johnson nonetheless had no intention of permitting Goldwater to usurp the role of defending America's pride and patriotism. The single bombing raid against Communist attackers of United States ships provided an ideal opportunity. He was able to demonstrate that the "man of peace" was not a man of weakness or timidity. And on the verge of the campaign, the Tonkin affair allowed this consensus President to speak by his actions to each of his constituencies, satisfying all of them in one stroke.

But the rhetoric of restrained commitment to South Vietnam, so effective during the campaign, later provoked serious difficulties when Johnson finally had to choose between massive escalation or the defeat of Saigon. As the country learned the less innocent reality of the United States role at the Gulf of Tonkin and saw hundreds of thousands of their fellow Americans being sent to war, millions of Americans came to feel that the President had betrayed them, lied, and deliberately tricked them to get their votes.

"The virtues of the politician," Hans Morgenthau writes, "can easily become vices when they are brought to bear upon the statesman's task." The politician, Johnson's experience had taught him, could make promises without keeping them; words spoken in public had little relation to the practical conduct of daily life. But whatever justification a politician may claim for deceptions, the statesman must align his words with his action.

At the time, however, Johnson's action at the Gulf of Tonkin, along with his campaign statements, constituted a political master stroke. Though some uneasiness about Vietnam was reflected in letters to the editor in a few papers, in the two lonely Senate votes against the Tonkin Resolution, and in a handful of demonstrations and peace rallies, the American people and their politicians praised Johnson for the feat of riding two horses in different directions at the same time. Some wanted peace, even at the price of withdrawal. Some wanted victory, even at the price of a wider war. Others wanted, if not victory, at least to avoid defeat while keeping the peace. And most did not want to pay attention to the issue.

QUESTIONS TO CONSIDER

1. What assumptions about Communism shaped Johnson's policy in Vietnam?

2. Why did Johnson put off making decisions in Vietnam until late 1964?

3. What was the significance of the Tonkin Gulf Resolution?

4. "The virtues of the politician can easily become vices when they are brought to bear upon the stateman's task." What did Hans Morgenthau mean by this statement, and how does it apply to Johnson's decisions in Vietnam?

5. How did the role of the President in foreign affairs change from Washington's time to Johnson's time? How has it changed from Washington's time to the present?

World Leader

The Roosevelt Corollary to the Monroe Doctrine Citing the Monroe Doctrine, Theodore Roosevelt urged Congress to get tough with any European powers that might use force to recover money loaned in Latin America. He argued that interference could require the United States to exercise "an international police power" to protect its economic interests.

▲
Roosevelt with his son Kermit. His letter to Kermit about politics and
world affairs is on page 129.

◀ **Big Stick Policy** Roosevelt based his foreign policy on a West
African proverb, "Speak softly and carry a big stick; you will go far."

◀ **Allies Confer** During World War President Franklin Roosevelt met with Allied leaders to discuss steps in the plans to invade Europe and defeat Japan. Here in 1943 in Casablanca, Roosevelt reviews the statement that he and British Prim Minister Winston Churchill (seated on the right) would issue following their meeting.

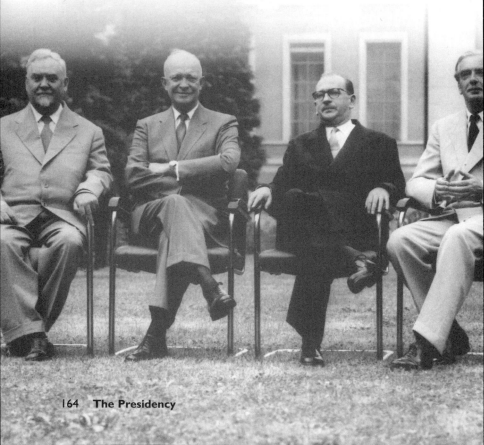

▲

Berlin Crisis President John F. Kennedy (1961–1963) and West German Chancellor Konrad Adenauer tour the German city of Berlin, divided since the Second World War. On returning home, Kennedy pledged to the American people that "we cannot and will not permit the Communists to drive us out of Berlin." Soviet Premier Khrushchev's response was to build a huge concrete wall topped by barbed wire to separate the two halves of the city.

◀ **The Big Four** In 1955, President Dwight Eisenhower (1953–1961) took an active role in handling the tensions of the Cold War. Here he is shown with Soviet Premier Nikolai Bulganin on his left, and French Premiere Andre Fauré and British Prime Minister Sir Anthony Eden on his right.

▲

The Ghosts of War President Lyndon B. Johnson (1963–1969) expanded the United States' role in the Vietnam War. The unpopularity of the war forced him to withdraw his name from consideration for a second term of office in the election of 1968. Here, artist Paul Michael Szep shows Johnson haunted by ghosts of the war.

Nixon in China In 1972, President Richard Nixon (1969–1974) made diplomatic history as the first U.S. President to visit China. His meetings with top Chinese officials, including the legendary Mao Zedong (shown here), led to a thaw in Cold War relations between the two countries. Shortly after the trip, the U.S. finally recognized the mainland Chinese government as legitimate, ending a twenty-three year freeze in relations between the nations. ▶

▲
Peace in the Middle East In 1979, President Jimmy Carter (1977–1981) facilitated a historic peace treaty between Egyptian president Anwar el-Sadat (shown here on the left) and Israel's prime minister Menachem Begin (on the right).

American Interests in the Gulf War When, in 1990, Iraq invaded Kuwait and its oil fields and threatened Saudi Arabia, President George Bush sought the support of the United Nations and of Congress to fight back. Here in the White House with Vice President Dan Quayle (right), Bush manages the crisis just minutes after the war began.
▼

Presidential
Character

Part four

The Presidential Character

BY JAMES DAVID BARBER

By the close of the twentieth century, forty-one men had served as President of the United States. They all had different priorities, personalities, and styles, and some are considered to have been more successful than others. What do Presidents have in common? Is it possible to identify the qualities that propelled these men to the highest political position in the country? In his controversial book, The Presidential Character, *James David Barber argues that the personal qualities of a President have a tremendous effect upon his performance in the White House. Character is shaped in childhood, and as an individual grows up, his or her world view and style develop on the foundation set in earlier years. Barber, a noted scholar of the presidency, maintains that a President's approach to power and his expectations of others in turn are determined by character development earlier in life.*

When a citizen votes for a presidential candidate he makes, in effect, a prediction. He chooses from among the contenders the one he thinks (or feels, or guesses) would be the best President. He operates in a situation of immense uncertainty. If he has a long voting history, he can recall time and time again when he guessed wrong. He listens to the commentators, the politicians, and his friends, then adds it all up in some rough way to produce his prediction and his vote. Earlier in the game, his anticipations have been taken into account, either directly in the polls and primaries or indirectly in the minds of politicians who want to nominate someone he will like. But he must choose in the midst of a cloud of confusion, a rain of phony advertising, a storm of sermons, a hail of complex issues, a fog of **charisma**[1] and boredom, and a thunder of accusation and defense. In the face of this chaos, a great many citizens fall back on the past, vote their old allegiances, and let it go at that. Nevertheless, the citizen's vote says that on balance he expects Mr. X would outshine Mr. Y in the presidency.

This [book] is meant to help citizens and those who advise them cut through the confusion and get at some clear criteria for choosing Presidents. To understand what actual Presidents do and what potential Presidents might do, the first need is to see the man whole—not as some abstract **embodiment**[2] of civic virtue, some score-card of issue stands, or some reflection of a faction, but as a human being like the rest of us, a person trying to cope with a difficult environment. To that task he brings his own character, his own view of the world, his own political style. None of that is new for him. If we can see the pattern he has set for his political life we can, I contend, estimate much better his pattern as he confronts the stresses and chances of the presidency.

---

[1] **charisma**—magnetic personal quality that inspires loyalty and devotion.
[2] **embodiment**—image.

The presidency is a peculiar office. The founding fathers left it extraordinarily loose in definition, partly because they trusted George Washington to invest a tradition as he went along. It is an institution made a piece at a time by successive men in the White House. Jefferson reached out to Congress to put together the beginnings of political parties; Jackson's dramatic force extended electoral **partisanship**[3] to its mass base; Lincoln vastly expanded the administrative reach of the office, Wilson and the Roosevelts showed its **rhetorical**[4] possibilities—in fact every President's mind and demeanor has left its mark on a heritage still in lively development.

But the presidency is much more than an institution. It is a focus of feelings. In general, popular feelings about politics are low-key, shallow, casual. For example, the vast majority of Americans knows virtually nothing of what Congress is doing and cares less. The presidency is different. The presidency is the focus for the most intense and persistent emotions in the American polity. The President is a symbolic leader, the one figure who draws together the people's hopes and fears for the political future. On top of all his routine duties, he has to carry that off—or fail.

Our emotional attachment to Presidents shows up when one dies in office. People were not just disappointed or worried when President Kennedy was killed; people wept at the loss of a man most had never even met. Kennedy was young and charismatic—but history shows that whenever a President dies in office, heroic Lincoln or **debased**[5] Harding, McKinley or Garfield, the same wave of deep emotion sweeps across the country. On the other hand, the death of an ex-President brings forth no such intense emotional reaction.

---

[3] **partisanship**—state in which strong party loyalties dominate.

[4] **rhetorical**—related to persuasive speech and writing.

[5] **debased**—disgraced.

The President is the first political figure children are aware of (later they add Congress, the Court, and others, as "helpers" of the President). With some exceptions among children in deprived circumstances, the President is seen as a "benevolent leader," one who nurtures, sustains, and inspires the citizenry. Presidents regularly show up among "most admired" contemporaries and forebears, and the President is the "best known" (in the sense of sheer name recognition) person in the country. At inauguration time, even Presidents elected by close margins are supported by much larger majorities than the election returns show, for people rally round as he actually assumes office. There is a similar reaction when the people see their President threatened by crisis: if he takes action, there is a favorable spurt in the Gallup poll whether he succeeds or fails.

Obviously the President gets more attention in schoolbooks, press, and television than any other politician. He is one of very few who can make news by doing good things. His emotional state is a matter of continual public commentary, as is the manner in which his personal and official families conduct themselves. The media bring across the President not as some neutral administrator or corporate executive to be assessed by his production, but as a special being with mysterious dimensions.

We have no king. The sentiments English children— and adults—direct to the Queen have no place to go in our system but to the President. Whatever his talents— Coolidge-type or Roosevelt-type—the President is the only available object for such national-religious-monarchical sentiments as Americans possess.

The President helps people make sense of politics. Congress is a tangle of committees, the bureaucracy is a maze of agencies. The President is one man trying to do a job—a picture much more understandable to the mass of people who find themselves in the same boat.

Furthermore, he is the top man. He ought to know what is going on and set it right. So when the economy goes sour, or war drags on, or domestic violence erupts, the President is available to take the blame. Then when things go right, it seems the President must have had a hand in it. Indeed, the flow of political life is marked off by Presidents: the "Eisenhower Era," the "Kennedy Years."

What all this means is that the President's *main* responsibilities reach far beyond administering the Executive Branch or commanding the armed forces. The White House is first and foremost a place of public leadership. That inevitably brings to bear on the President intense moral, sentimental, and quasi-religious[6] pressures which can, if he lets them, distort his own thinking and feeling. If there is such a thing as extraordinary sanity, it is needed nowhere so much as in the White House.

Who the President is at a given time can make a profound difference in the whole thrust and direction of national politics. Since we have only one President at a time, we can never prove this by comparison, but even the most superficial speculation confirms the common sense view that the man himself weighs heavily among other historical factors. . . .

The burden of this [argument] is that the crucial differences can be anticipated by an understanding of a potential President's character, his world view, and his style. This kind of prediction is not easy; well-informed observers often have guessed wrong as they watched a man step toward the White House. One thinks of Woodrow Wilson, the scholar who would bring reason to politics; of Herbert Hoover, the Great Engineer who would organize chaos into progress; of Franklin D. Roosevelt, that champion of the balanced budget; of

---

[6] quasi-religious—almost religious; religious-like.

Harry Truman, whom the office would surely over-whelm; of Dwight D. Eisenhower, militant crusader; of John F. Kennedy, who would lead beyond moralisms to achievements; of Lyndon B. Johnson, the Southern conservative; and of Richard M. Nixon, conciliator.[7] Spotting the errors is easy. Predicting with even approximate accuracy is going to require some sharp tools and close attention in their use. But the experiment is worth it because the question is critical and because it lends itself to correction by evidence.

My argument comes in layers.

First, a President's personality is an important shaper of his presidential behavior on nontrivial matters.

Second, presidential personality is patterned. His character, world view, and style fit together in a dynamic package understandable in psychological terms.

Third, a President's personality interacts with the power situation he faces and the national "climate of expectations" dominant at the time he serves. The tuning, the **resonance**[8]—or lack of it—between these external factors and his personality sets in motion the dynamics of his presidency.

Fourth, the best way to predict a President's character, world view, and style is to see how they were put together in the first place. That happened in his early life, culminating in his first independent political success.

But the core of the argument . . . is that presidential character—the basic stance a man takes toward his presidential experience—comes in four varieties. The most important thing to know about a President or candidate is where he fits among these types, defined according to

---

[7] This list of predictions from Woodrow Wilson through Richard Nixon includes real descriptors of the men, but anticipates results they did not achieve.

[8] **resonance**—reverberation; movement that produces results.

(a) how active he is and (b) whether or not he gives the impression he enjoys his political life.

Let me spell out these concepts briefly before getting down to cases.

Personality Shapes Performance

I am not about to argue that once you know a President's personality you know everything. But as the cases will demonstrate, the degree and quality of a President's emotional involvement in an issue are powerful influences on how he defines the issue itself, how much attention he pays to it, which facts and persons he sees as relevant to its resolution, and finally, what principles and purposes he associates with the issue. Every story of presidential decision-making is really two stories: an outer one in which a rational man calculates and an inner one in which an emotional man feels. The two are forever connected. Any real President is one whole man and his deeds reflect his wholeness.

As for personality, it is a matter of tendencies. It is not that one President "has" some basic characteristic that another President does not "have." That old way of treating a trait as a possession, like a rock in a basket, ignores the universality of aggressiveness, compliancy, detachment, and other human drives. We all have all of them but in different amounts and in different combinations.

The Pattern of Character, World View, and Style

The most visible part of the pattern is style. Style *is the President's habitual way of performing his three political roles: rhetoric, personal relations, and homework.* Not to be confused with "stylishness," charisma, or appearance, style is how the President goes about doing what the office requires him to do—to speak, directly or through media, to large audiences; to deal face to face with other politicians, individually and in small, relatively private groups; and to read, write, and calculate by himself in order to manage the endless flow of details that stream onto his desk. No President can escape doing at least some of each. But there are marked differences in stylistic emphasis from President to President. The *balance* among the three style elements varies; one President may put most of himself into rhetoric, another may stress close, informal dealing, while still another may devote his energies mainly to study and **cogitation**.[9] Beyond the balance, we want to see each President's peculiar habits of style, his mode of coping with and adapting to these presidential demands. For example, I think both Calvin Coolidge and John F. Kennedy were primarily **rhetoricians**,[10] but they went about it in contrasting ways.

A President's *world view consists of his primary, politically relevant beliefs, particularly his conceptions of social causality,*[11] *human nature, and the central moral conflicts of the time.* This is how he sees the world and his lasting opinions about what he sees. Style is his way of acting; world view is his way of seeing. Like the rest of us, a President develops over a lifetime certain conceptions of reality—how things work in politics, what people are like, what the main purposes are. These assumptions or conceptions help him make sense of his world, give some semblance of order to the chaos of existence. Perhaps most important: a man's world view affects what he pays attention to, and a great deal of politics is about paying attention. The name of the game for many politicians is not so much "Do this, do that" as it is "Look here!"...

---

[9] **cogitation**—earnest thought or consideration; reflection.

[10] **rhetoricians**—politicians who use memorable, vivid language in their speeches.

[11] *social causality*—the connection between the causes of problems or actions in society and their effects.

Character, world view, and style are abstractions from the reality of the whole individual. In every case they form an integrated pattern: the man develops a combination which makes psychological sense for him, a dynamic arrangement of motives, beliefs, and habits in the service of his need for self-esteem.

The Power Situation and "Climate of Expectations"

Presidential character resonates with the political situation the President faces. It adapts him as he tries to adapt it. The support he has from the public and interest groups, the party balance in Congress, the thrust of Supreme Court opinion together set the basic power situation he must deal with. An activist President may run smack into a brick wall of resistance, then pull back and wait for a better moment. On the other hand, a President who sees himself as a quiet caretaker may not try to exploit even the most favorable power situation. So it is the relationship between President and the political configuration that makes the system tick.

Even before public opinion polls, the President's real or supposed popularity was a large factor in his performance. Besides the power mix in Washington, the President has to deal with a national climate of expectations, the predominant needs thrust up to him by the people. There are at least three recurrent themes around which these needs are focused.

People look to the President for *reassurance*, a feeling that things will be all right, that the President will take care of his people. The psychological request is for a **surcease**[12] of anxiety. Obviously, modern life in America involves considerable doses of fear, tension, anxiety, worry; from time to time, the public mood calls for a rest, a time of peace, a breathing space, a "return to normalcy."

---

[12] **surcease**—end, completion.

Another theme is the demand for a sense of *progress and action*. The President ought to do something to direct the nation's course—or at least be in there pitching for the people. The President is looked to as a take-charge man, a doer, a turner of the wheels, a producer of progress—even if that means some sacrifice of serenity.

A third type of climate of expectations is the public need for a sense of *legitimacy*[13] from, and in, the presidency. The President should be a master politician who is above politics. He should have a right to his place and a rightful way of acting in it. The respectability —even religiosity—of the office has to be protected by a man who presents himself as defender of the faith. There is more to this than dignity, more than propriety. The President is expected to personify our betterness in an inspiring way, to express in what he does and is (not just in what he says) a moral idealism which, in much of the public mind, is the very opposite of "politics."

Over time the climate of expectations shifts and changes. Wars, depressions, and other national events contribute to that change, but there also is a rough cycle, from an emphasis on action (which begins to look too "political") to an emphasis on legitimacy (the moral uplift of which creates its own strains) to an emphasis on reassurance and rest (which comes to seem like drift) and back to action again. One need not be astrological about it. The point is that the climate of expectations at any given time is the political air the President has to breathe. Relating to this climate is a large part of his task.

Predicting Presidents

The best way to predict a President's character, world view, and style is to see how he constructed them in the first place. Especially in the early stages, life is

---

[13] *legitimacy*—rightness; authority.

experimental; consciously or not, a person tries out various ways of defining and maintaining and raising self-esteem. He looks to his environment for clues as to who he is and how well he is doing. These lessons of life slowly sink in: certain self-images and evaluations, certain ways of looking at the world, certain styles of action get confirmed by his experience and he gradually adopts them as his own. If we can see that process of development, we can understand the product. The features to note are those bearing on presidential performance.

Experimental development continues all the way to death; we will not blind ourselves to midlife changes, particularly in the full-scale prediction case, that of Richard Nixon. But it is often much easier to see the basic patterns in early life histories. Later on a whole host of distractions—especially the image-making all politicians learn to practice—clouds the picture.

In general, character has its *main* development in childhood, world view in adolescence, style in early adulthood. The stance toward life I call character grows out of the child's experiments in relating to parents, brothers and sisters, and peers at play and in school, as well as to his own body and the objects around it. Slowly the child defines an orientation toward experience; once established, that tends to last despite much subsequent contradiction. By adolescence, the child has been hearing and seeing how people make their worlds meaningful, and now he is moved to relate himself—his own meanings—to those around him. His focus of attention shifts toward the future; he senses that decisions about his fate are coming and he looks into the **premises**[14] for those decisions. Thoughts about the way the world works and how one might work in it, about

---

[14] **premises**—assumptions.

what people are like and how one might be like them or not, and about the values people share and how one might share in them too—these are typical concerns for the post-child, pre-adult mind of the adolescent.

These themes come together strongly in early adulthood, when the person moves from contemplation to responsible action and adopts a style. In most biographical accounts this period stands out in stark clarity—the time of emergence, the time the young man found himself. I call it his first independent political success. It was then he moved beyond the detailed guidance of his family; then his self-esteem was dramatically boosted; then he came forth as a person to be reckoned with by other people. The *way* he did that is profoundly important to him. Typically he grasps that style and hangs onto it. Much later, coming into the presidency, something in him remembers this earlier victory and reemphasizes the style that made it happen.

Character provides the main thrust and broad direction—but it does not *determine*, in any fixed sense, world view and style. The story of development does not end with the end of childhood. Thereafter, the culture one grows in and the ways that culture is translated by parents and peers shape the meanings one makes of his character. The going world view gets learned and that learning helps channel character forces. Thus it will not necessarily be true that compulsive characters have reactionary beliefs, or that compliant characters believe in compromise. Similarly for style: historical accidents play a large part in furnishing special opportunities for action—and in blocking off alternatives. For example, however much anger a young man may feel, that anger will not be expressed in rhetoric unless and until his life situation provides a platform and an audience. Style thus has a stature and independence of its own. Those who would reduce all explanation to character neglect these highly significant later channelings. For beyond the root is the branch, above the foundation the super-structure, and starts do not prescribe finishes.

Four Types of Presidential Character

The five concepts—character, world view, style, power situation, and climate of expectations—run through the accounts of Presidents in [later chapters of Barber's book], which cluster the Presidents since Theodore Roosevelt into four types. This is the fundamental scheme of the study. It offers a way to move past the complexities to the main contrasts and comparisons.

The first baseline in defining presidential types is *activity-passivity*. How much energy does the man invest in his presidency? Lyndon Johnson went at his day like a human cyclone, coming to rest long after the sun went down. Calvin Coolidge often slept eleven hours a night and still needed a nap in the middle of the day. In between the Presidents array themselves on the high or low side of the activity line.

The second baseline is *positive-negative affect*[15] toward one's activity—this is, how he feels about what he does. Relatively speaking, does he seem to experience his political life as happy or sad, enjoyable or discouraging, positive or negative in its main effect? The feeling I am after here is not grim satisfaction in a job well done, not some philosophical conclusion. The idea is this: is he someone who, on the surfaces we can see, gives forth the feeling that he has *fun* in political life? Franklin Roosevelt's Secretary of War, Henry L. Stimson, wrote that the Roosevelts "not only understood the *use* of power, they knew the *enjoyment* of power, too. . . . Whether a man is burdened by power or enjoys power; whether he is trapped by responsibility or made free by

---

[15] *affect*—emotional content.

it; whether he is moved by other people and outer forces or moves them—that is the essence of leadership."

The positive-negative baseline, then, is a general symptom of the fit between the man and his experience, a kind of register of *felt* satisfaction. Why might we expect these two simple dimensions to outline the main character types? Because they stand for two central features of anyone's orientation toward life. In nearly every study of personality, some form of the active-passive contrast is critical; the general tendency to act or be acted upon is evident in such concepts as dominance-submission, **extraversion-introversion**,[16] aggression-timidity, attack-defense, fight-flight, engagement-withdrawal, approach-avoidance. In everyday life we sense quickly the general energy output of the people we deal with. Similarly we catch on fairly quickly to the affect dimension—whether the person seems to be optimistic or pessimistic, hopeful or **skeptical**,[17] happy or sad. The two baselines are clear and they are also independent of one another: all of us know people who are very active but seem discouraged, others who are quite passive but seem happy, and so forth. The activity baseline refers to what one does, the affect baseline to how one feels about what he does.

Both are crude clues to character. They are leads into four basic character patterns long familiar in psychological research. In summary form, these are the main configurations:

Active-positive: There is a **congruence**,[18] a consistency, between much activity and the enjoyment of it, indicating relatively high self-esteem and relative success in relating to the environment. The man shows an orientation

[16] **extraversion-introversion**—outgoing vs. a withdrawn personality.
[17] **skeptical**—doubting.
[18] **congruence**—coming together; accord.

toward productiveness as a value and an ability to use his styles flexibly, adaptively, suiting the dance to the music. He sees himself as developing over time toward relatively well defined personal goals—growing toward his image of himself as he might yet be. There is an emphasis on rational mastery, on using the brain to move the feet. This may get him into trouble; he may fail to take account of the irrational in politics. Not everyone he deals with sees things his way and he may find it hard to understand why.

Active-negative: The contradiction here is between relatively intense effort and relatively low emotional reward for that effort. The activity has a compulsive quality, as if the man were trying to make up for something or to escape from anxiety into hard work. He seems ambitious, striving upward, power-seeking. His stance toward the environment is aggressive and he has a persistent problem in managing his aggressive feelings. His self-image is vague and **discontinuous**.[19] Life is a hard struggle to achieve and hold power, hampered by the condemnations of a perfectionistic conscience. Active-negative types pour energy into the political system, but it is an energy distorted from within.

Passive-positive: This is the receptive, compliant, other-directed character whose life is a search for affection as a reward for being agreeable and cooperative rather than personally assertive. The contradiction is between low self-esteem (on grounds of being unlovable, unattractive) and a superficial optimism. A hopeful attitude helps dispel doubt and elicits encouragement from others. Passive-positive types help soften the harsh edges of politics. But their dependence and the fragility of their hopes and enjoyments make disappointment in politics likely.

---

[19] **discontinuous**—interrupted; not consistent.

Passive-negative: The factors are consistent—but how are we to account for the man's *political* role-taking? Why is someone who does little in politics and enjoys it less there at all? The answer lies in the passive-negative's character-rooted orientation toward doing dutiful service; this compensates for low self-esteem based on a sense of uselessness. Passive-negative types are in politics because they think they ought to be. They may be well adapted to certain nonpolitical roles, but they lack the experience and flexibility to perform effectively as political leaders. Their tendency is to withdraw, to escape from the conflict and uncertainty of politics by emphasizing vague principles (especially prohibitions) and procedural arrangements. They become guardians of the right and proper way, above the sordid politicking of lesser men.

Active-positive presidents want most to achieve results. Active-negatives aim to get and keep power. Passive-positives are after love. Passive-negatives emphasize their civic virtue. The relation of activity to enjoyment in a President thus tends to outline a cluster of characteristics, to set apart the adapted from the **compulsive**,[20] compliant, and withdrawn types.

The first four Presidents of the United States, conveniently, ran through this gamut of character types. (Remember, we are talking about tendencies, broad directions; no individual man exactly fits a category.) George Washington—clearly the most important President in the **pantheon**[21]—established the fundamental legitimacy of an American government at a time when this was a matter in considerable question.

---

[20] **compulsive**—obsessive.

[21] **pantheon**—all the gods collectively. Barber uses this term, from Greek mythology, to refer to the original four Presidents who seem to be distant, almost mythical, bigger-than-life figures.

Washington's dignity, **judiciousness**,[22] his aloof air of reserve and dedication to duty fit the passive-negative or withdrawing type best. Washington did not seek innovation, he sought stability. He longed to retire to Mount Vernon, but fortunately was persuaded to stay on through a second term, in which, by rising above the political conflict between Hamilton and Jefferson and inspiring confidence in his own integrity, he gave the nation time to develop the organized means for peaceful change.

John Adams followed, a **dour**[23] New England Puritan, much given to work and worry, an impatient and **irascible**[24] man—an active-negative President, a compulsive type. Adams was far more partisan than Washington; the survival of the system through his presidency demonstrated that the nation could tolerate, for a time, domination by one of its **nascent**[25] political parties. As President, an angry Adams brought the United States to the brink of war with France, and presided over the new nation's first experiment in political repression: the Alien and Sedition Acts, forbidding, among other things, unlawful [associations] "with intent to oppose any measure or measures of the government of the United States," or "any false, scandalous, and malicious writing or writings against the United States, or the President of the United States, with intent to defame . . . or to bring them or either of them, into contempt or disrepute."

Then came Jefferson. He too had his troubles and failures—in the design of national defense, for example. As for his presidential character (only one element in success or failure), Jefferson was clearly active-positive.

---

[22] **judiciousness**—wisdom.

[23] **dour**—sullenly gloomy; grim.

[24] **irascible**—bad-tempered.

[25] **nascent**—newborn.

A child of the Enlightenment, he applied his reason to organizing connections with Congress aimed at strengthening the more popular forces. A man of **catholic**[26] interests and delightful humor, Jefferson combined a clear and open vision of what the country could be with a profound political sense, expressed in his famous phrase, "Every difference of opinion is not a difference of principle."

The fourth President was James Madison, "Little Jemmy," the constitutional philosopher thrown into the White House at a time of great international turmoil. Madison comes closest to the passive-positive, or compliant, type; he suffered from irresolution, tried to compromise his way out, and gave in too readily to the "warhawks" urging combat with Britain. The nation drifted into war, and Madison wound up ineptly commanding his collection of amateur generals in the streets of Washington. General Jackson's victory at New Orleans saved the Madison administration's historical reputation; but he left the presidency with the United States close to bankruptcy and secession.

These four Presidents—like all Presidents—were persons trying to cope with the roles they had won by using the equipment they had built over a lifetime. The President is not some shapeless organism in a flood of novelties, but a man with a memory in a system with a history. Like all of us, he draws on his past to shape his future. The pathetic hope that the White House will turn a Caligula into a Marcus Aurelius[27] is as naive as the fear that ultimate power inevitably corrupts. The problem is to understand—and to state understandably—what in the personal past foreshadows the presidential future. . . .

---

[26] **catholic**—universal; broad.

[27] Caligula and Marcus Aurelius were two emperors of ancient Rome. The first was a cruel tyrant and the second a great and noble leader.

QUESTIONS TO CONSIDER

1. How does Barber define the character, world view, and style of a President? At what stage of life does each develop?

2. What are the three types of climates of expectations that people place on the President?

3. What are the four types of presidential character? Explain in your own words.

4. Choose one of the Presidents. How did his character affect the role he played as a world leader?

Letter to a Namesake

BY THOMAS JEFFERSON

Thomas Jefferson wrote to Thomas Jefferson Smith, a friend's son who had been named for the former President, in 1825. It was only a little more than a year before Jefferson's death. The letter provides rare insight into the personal qualities most valued by our third President (1801–1809).

Monticello, February 21, 1825

This letter will, to you, be as one from the dead. The writer will be in the grave before you can weigh its **counsels.**[1] Your affectionate and excellent father has requested that I would address to you something which might possibly have a favorable influence on the course of life you have to run, and I too, as a namesake, feel an

---

[1] **counsels**—advice.

interest in that course. Few words will be necessary, with good **dispositions**[2] on your part. Adore God. Reverence and cherish your parents. Love your neighbor as yourself, and your country more than yourself. Be just. Be true. Murmur not at the ways of **Providence**.[3] So shall the life into which you have entered, be the **portal**[4] to one of eternal and **ineffable**[5] bliss. And if to the dead it is permitted to care for the things of this world, every action of your life will be under my regard. Farewell.

The portrait of a good man by the most sublime of poets,[6] for your imitation.

Lord, who's the happy man that may to thy blest courts **repair**;[7]
Not stranger-like to visit them but to inhabit there?
'Tis he whose every thought and deed by rules of virtue moves;
Whose generous tongue **disdains**[8] to speak the thing his heart disproves.
Who never did a slander forge, his neighbor's fame to wound;
Nor **hearken**[9] to a false report, by malice whispered round.
Who vice in all its pomp and power, can treat with just neglect;

---

[2] **dispositions**—attitudes; tendencies.

[3] **Providence**—fate; God.

[4] **portal**—entry.

[5] **ineffable**—undescribably or unutterably sacred; heavenly.

[6] most sublime of poets—David, the traditional author of the psalms in the Bible. This is Psalm 15.

[7] **repair**—return.

[8] **disdains**—refuses.

[9] **hearken**—listen.

And piety, though clothed in rags, religiously respect.

Who to his **plighted**[10] vows and trust has ever firmly
  stood;

And though he promise to his loss, he makes his
  promise good.

Whose soul in **usury**[11] disdains his treasure to employ;

Whom no rewards can ever bribe the guiltless to
  destroy.

The man, who, by his steady course, has happiness
  insur'd.

When earth's foundations shake, shall stand, by
  Providence secur'd.

A Decalogue[12] of Canons[13] for observation in practical life.

1. Never put off till to-morrow what you can do
   to-day.

2. Never trouble another for what you can do yourself.

3. Never spend your money before you have it.

4. Never buy what you do not want because it is
   cheap; it will be dear to you.

5. Pride costs us more than hunger, thirst and cold.

6. We never repent of having eaten too little.

7. Nothing is troublesome that we do willingly.

8. How much pain have cost us the evils which have
   never happened.

---

[10] **plighted**—pledged.

[11] **usury**—high rate of interest charged on a debt.

[12] Decalogue—set of rules, such as the Ten Commandments.

[13] Canons—desirable actions.

9. Take things always by their smooth handle.

10. When angry, count ten, before you speak; if very angry, an hundred.

Thomas Jefferson

QUESTIONS TO CONSIDER

1. How would you describe the person that Jefferson presents to the young man as a role model?

2. Would a person with the qualities that Jefferson praises make a good President? Why or why not?

3. In your opinion, is Jefferson's advice out of date? Explain.

The Gettysburg Address

BY PRESIDENT ABRAHAM LINCOLN

Great Presidents are often remembered for their special insight regarding the nation's past and their rare vision of the future. Never was such understanding more clearly evident than in these famous words of President Abraham Lincoln (1861–1865), which he spoke in July 1864 at the dedication of a military cemetery on the first anniversary of the Battle of Gettysburg, one of the Civil War's bloodiest and most important fights. Legend has it that Lincoln wrote the brief speech on the back of an envelope while traveling by train to Gettysburg. Whatever the truth of that, it is clear that the President did not think much of the speech himself, and it was largely ignored by the newspapers that covered the dedication ceremony. The speech now is regarded as a masterpiece, one of the most famous ever written.

Four score[1] and seven years ago our fathers brought forth on this continent a new nation, conceived in liberty

---

[1] **Four score**—eighty.

and dedicated to the **proposition**[2] that all men are created equal. Now we are engaged in a great civil war, testing whether that nation or any nation so conceived and so dedicated can long endure. We are met on a great battlefield of that war. We have come to dedicate a portion of that field as a final resting-place for those who here gave their lives that that nation might live. It is altogether fitting and proper that we should do this. But in a larger sense, we cannot dedicate, we cannot **consecrate**,[3] we cannot hallow this ground. The brave men, living and dead, who struggled here have consecrated it far above our poor power to add or detract. The world will little note nor long remember what we say here, but it can never forget what they did here. It is for us the living rather to be dedicated here to the unfinished work which they who fought here have thus far so nobly advanced. It is rather for us to be here dedicated to the great task remaining before us—that from these honored dead we take increased devotion to that cause for which they gave the last full measure of devotion—that we here highly resolve that these dead shall not have died in vain, that this nation under God shall have a new birth of freedom, and that government of the people, by the people, for the people shall not perish from the earth.

---

[2] **proposition**—theory.
[3] **consecrate**—bless.

QUESTIONS TO CONSIDER

1. According to Lincoln, what was the "unfinished work" of those who fought at Gettysburg?

2. What is Lincoln's vision for the country when the Civil War is ended? How might fighting the war lead to his goals?

3. Does the Gettysburg Address deserve its reputation for greatness? Why or why not?

Presidential Qualities

George Washington (1789–1797) The calm, reassuring "father" of the country brought stability during the insecure years of the founding of the United States. He presided over bitter debates and conflicts, keeping the young nation together at a critical point in history. He brought poise, wisdom, and dignity to the office of President.

▲

John Adams (1797–1801) This highly involved patriot of the American independence movement against Britain could be personally abrasive and rude in his treatment of others. His personal qualities and highly criticized policies contributed to his unpopularity as the second President, but he still is widely admired for his unyielding dedication to his beliefs.

▲
Thomas Jefferson (1801–1809) This multi-talented Virginia aristocrat is known for his strong belief in the ability of ordinary individuals to participate in democracy. He rejected any semblance of the President as king and even walked to his own inauguration in 1801. As President, he simplified public ceremonies and reduced expenses.

▲

James Madison (1809–1817) This quiet, well-reasoned President's main contribution came before he assumed office. His genius for compromise worked best in his writing of the Constitution at the Convention in 1787 and his defense of it in the renowned *Federalist Papers*. Without his work, the Constitution might not have been ratified. However, during his presidency, this quality was interpreted by some as weakness, and Senate "war hawks" pressed for declaration of the War of 1812 against Britain, an unnecessary and nearly disastrous action.

▲

Lincoln at Gettysburg The little speech that Abraham Lincoln (1861–1865) gave at the dedication of a National Soldiers' Cemetery—it was only ten sentences and took him about five minutes to deliver—has become a classic hymn to the principles of freedom and democracy that are worth struggling and dying for.

▲
Theodore Roosevelt to Students On a trip across the country in 1903 to learn the views of the people, Roosevelt gave a talk at Northwestern University in Evanston, Illinois. "Intellectual supremacy is good," he said, "physical prowess desirable; but better than all, and without which none can succeed, is an upright character."

from

This I Remember

BY ELEANOR ROOSEVELT

Eleanor Roosevelt is widely known as one of the most influential "First Ladies" in American history. In this excerpt, she reflects on the character of her late husband, Franklin Roosevelt, who was President from 1933 to 1945. She also reveals a great deal of her own character, reinforcing the basis for her larger-than-life reputation.

I do not claim that I can be entirely objective about him, but there are some things I know that I feel sure nobody else can know. Although no human being ever completely knows another human being, one cannot live for many years with a person without learning something about him. Other people may know certain sides of Franklin's character or particular facets of his personality better than I; but if I can contribute what I have learned and what I believe to be true, I may help to fill in the true picture for future historians.

The few books that have already been written about Franklin show quite plainly that everyone writes from his own point of view, and that a man like my husband, who was particularly **susceptible**[1] to people, took color from[2] whomever he was with, giving to each one something different of himself. Because he disliked being disagreeable, he made an effort to give each person who came in contact with him the feeling that he understood what his particular interest was. Frances Perkins,[3] in her book, has drawn a wonderful picture of him that in many respects no one else could possibly have drawn. Yet even in her book, I think, there are little inaccuracies and misinterpretations, arising from the fact that each of us brings to any contact with another person our own personality and our own interests and prejudices and beliefs.

Often people have told me that they were misled by Franklin. Even when they have not said it in so many words, I have sometimes felt that he left them, after an interview, with the idea that he was in entire agreement with them. I would know quite well, however, that he was not and that they would be very much surprised when later his actions were in complete contradiction to what they thought his attitude would be.

This misunderstanding not only arose from his dislike of being disagreeable, but from the interest that he always had in somebody else's point of view and his willingness to listen to it. If he thought it was well expressed and clear, he nodded his head and frequently said, "I see," or something of the sort. This did not mean that he was convinced of the truth of the arguments, or even that he entirely understood them, but only that he appreciated the way in which they were presented.

There is another fact which few people realize: the President of the United States gets more all-round infor-

---

[1] **susceptible**—open.

[2] took color from—adapted to.

[3] Frances Perkins—Roosevelt's Secretary of Labor, the first woman to be appointed to a cabinet post.

mation than most of the people who come to see him, though any one of them may know his own subject better than the President does. The President, however, must have a general outlook which takes in overall considerations; whereas other people think primarily about their own ideas, plans and responsibilities for the specific thing they hope to accomplish. This circumstance puts on a President the responsibility of gathering all possible points of view, of hearing very often conflicting ideas on a given subject, and of then making a final decision. It is one of the most difficult things a President has to do.

In addition, the fact that he can never have a personal loyalty greater than his loyalty to the nation sometimes makes it seem as though he were disloyal to his friends; but a man holding the office of President of the United States must think first of what he considers the greatest good of the people and the country.

As time went on, I think Franklin often felt that he must save himself from the strain of argument, and that his obligation to the people who came to see him was discharged when he took the time out of a very strenuous program to sit and listen. I know he always gave thought to what people said, but I have never known anyone less really influenced by others. Though he asked for advice from a great many people, he simply wanted points of view which might help him to form his final decision if he had not reached one, and which he sifted through his own knowledge and feelings. But once he reached a decision, people flattered themselves if they thought they ever changed it.

Franklin often used me to get the reflection of other people's thinking because he knew I made it a point to see and talk with a variety of people. I did not need to go on lecture trips, or go to inspect projects in different parts of the country, but my husband knew that I would not be satisfied to be merely an official hostess. He often suggested that I interest myself in certain things, such as the homestead projects.[4] He knew that life would be very uninteresting to me if I did not feel I was accomplishing something. Therefore, for my sake, he was glad when he found that for a few weeks in spring and fall I could and did go on paid lecture trips. I knew that I would not plan such trips. I had definite commitments and had signed formal contracts; but when they were an obligation, I arranged my time so that they were possible. The trips took me to many places throughout the country to which otherwise I might never have gone.

Naturally these lecture trips gave me more money for things I wanted to do than my husband could afford to give me. At the same time, I felt that Franklin used whatever I brought back to him in the way of observations and information as a check against the many official reports which he received.

Very often, when some matter was being fought out with his advisers, he would bring up the question at dinner and bait me into giving an opinion by stating as his own a point of view with which he knew I would disagree. He would give me all the arguments which had been advanced to him, and I would try **vociferously**[5] and with heat to refute them.

I remember one occasion, though the subject of the argument has now been forgotten, when I became extremely **vehement**[6] and irritated. My husband smiled indulgently and repeated all the things that everyone else had said to him. The next day he asked Miss Thompson[7] if I could have tea in the West Hall in the White House for him and Robert Bingham, who was then our ambassador to London and about to return to

---

[4] homestead projects—efforts to improve the working and living conditions of coal miners.

[5] **vociferously**—loudly.

[6] **vehement**—angry.

[7] Miss Thompson—Eleanor Roosevelt's assistant.

his post. I dutifully served them with tea, fully expecting to sit and listen in silence to a discussion of questions with which I probably would not be in agreement. Instead, to my complete surprise, I heard Franklin telling Ambassador Bingham to act, not according to the arguments that he had given me, but according to the arguments that I had given him! Without giving me a glance or the satisfaction of batting an eyelash in my direction, he calmly stated as his own the policies and beliefs he had argued against the night before! To this day I have no idea whether he had simply used me as a sounding board, as he so often did, with the idea of getting the reaction of the person on the outside, or whether my arguments had been needed to fortify his decision and to clarify his own mind.

After Franklin became President, many people told me how much they disagreed with him and how they were going in for an interview prepared to tell him so in no uncertain terms. They went in, but if I had a chance to see them as they came out, they usually looked at me blandly and behaved as though they never had disagreed at all. Only now and then was someone honest enough to say he had not been able to put forward his own point of view—a difficulty due partly, I think, to the effect of Franklin's personality and partly to the person's awe of the office itself.

Franklin had the gift of being able to draw out the people whom he wished to draw out and to silence those with whom he was bored—and in both cases the people were greatly charmed. When he did not want to hear what somebody had to say, he had a way of telling stories and talking about something quite different. Everyone who worked with him had to learn how to handle this technique of his if they were not to find that the questions they wanted to ask, or that the opinion they wanted to state, never got into words because

Franklin talked so steadily and so interestingly that they forgot what they had come to say.

Of all his **intimates**[8] only a few, I think, ever really understood how it was that people sometimes thought he was in agreement with them when he was not, or had given his consent when really he had never contemplated giving it. I may have been able to help some people to this understanding. Louis Howe,[9] I think, always understood this trait in Franklin, and Frank Walker, Edward J. Flynn, Henry Morgenthau, Junior, and Bernard Baruch came to know it well. With none of these men was his own interest ever paramount. The interest of each was in my husband and in the work to be done and they could be very objective even when their own work was involved.

I was often supposed to be a great influence on my husband politically. Over and over again people wrote, crediting me with being responsible for his actions and even for some of his appointments. Frances Perkins' appointment to the cabinet is a case in point. As a matter of fact, I never even suggested her. She had worked with Franklin in New York State and was his own choice, though I was delighted when he named her and glad that he felt a woman should be recognized.

There were times when a list of names suggested for appointment, to serve as individuals or groups, would come out and there would be no woman's name on the list. Then I might go to my husband and say that I was very weary of reminding him to remind the members of his cabinet and his advisers that women were in existence, that they were a factor in the life of the nation and increasingly important politically. He always smiled and said: "Of course; I thought a woman's name had been put on the list. Have someone call up and say I feel

---

[8] **intimates**—close friends.
[9] Louis Howe—Franklin Roosevelt's assistant and special friend.

a woman should be recognized." As a result, I was sometimes asked for suggestions and then I would mention two or three names. Sometimes they were considered and sometimes they were not.

The political influence that was attributed to me was **nil**[10] where my husband was concerned, largely because I never made the slightest effort to do what I knew I could not do. If I felt strongly about anything I told Franklin, since he had the power to do things and I did not, but he did not always feel as I felt.

I have since discovered, of course, that a great many government people to whom I referred letters regarded them as a mandate requiring prompt attention. Evidently they thought that if what I suggested was not done, I would complain to my husband. As a matter of fact, all I ever expected was that they would be interested in accomplishing the things that should be accomplished, since government is supposed to serve the good of the people. I thought that every government official investigated complaints and gladly tried to correct injustices. I realize now that this was a rather naive idea, for it is apparent from what people have told me that it was often only fear of White House displeasure that set the wheels in motion. This was not true of many departments, but I suppose it is only natural that some of the older departments, where a number of civil service people feel entrenched, should not want to bother with new activities. Both Mr. Woodin and Mr. Morgenthau must have made great changes in the old Treasury Department management. The standards set, particularly after Mr. Morgenthau became Secretary of the Treasury, must have seemed alarming to some of the old types of civil service officials.

I felt very critical of civil service officials at times. When they have been in a department for a long while,

---

[10] **nil**—nonexistent.

they can make any change very difficult. Nevertheless, I think it is true that there are an astonishing number of people who want to serve their country and are willing to accept the modest security and low pay of a civil service employee simply because they feel that they are performing a patriotic service.

Consciously, as I have said, I never tried to exert any political influence on my husband or on anyone else in the government. However, one cannot live in a political atmosphere and study the actions of a good politician, which my husband was, without absorbing some **rudimentary**[11] facts about politics. From him I learned that a good politician is marked to a great extent by his sense of timing. He says the right thing at the right moment. Though the immediate reaction may be unfavorable, in the long run it turns out that what he said needed to be said at the time he said it. I do not mean that Franklin never made mistakes; most of the time, however, his judgment was good. He could watch with enormous patience as a situation developed and would wait for exactly the right moment to act or speak. The quarantine speech,[12] for instance, was delivered at a time when it was necessary that people be made to think. The meeting with [British Prime Minister] Winston Churchill at Argentina and the announcement of the Atlantic Charter came at a crucial point in the country's life; in the same way, the D-Day prayer[13] lifted the morale of the people at a moment when that kind of inspiration was most needed. Franklin was a practical politician. He could always be told why certain actions or appointments were politically advisable. Sometimes

---

[11] **rudimentary**—basic.

[12] the quarantine speech—a controversial speech given in 1940 (before U.S. entry into World War II) in which Franklin Roosevelt warned that the United States was being harmed by the conflicts abroad.

[13] D-Day prayer—an inspirational public prayer by the President, broadcast nationally, as U.S. troops and their allies invaded German-occupied France on D-Day, June 6, 1944.

he acted on this advice; on the other hand, he did many things and made many appointments against the advice of the party politicians, simply because he believed they would have a good effect on the nation as a whole. And he was almost always right. However, as a practical politician, he knew and accepted the fact that he had to work with the people who were a part of the Democratic party organization. I often heard him discuss the necessity and role of local political organizations, but he recognized that certain of them were a detriment to the party as a whole. He never got over his feeling against Tammany Hall[14] or any boss-ridden organization, though he acknowledged that some were well-administered and valuable.

---

[14] Tammany Hall—the famous Democratic party machine that dominated New York City at the turn of the twentieth century.

QUESTIONS TO CONSIDER

1. According to Eleanor Roosevelt, what were Franklin Roosevelt's best qualities?

2. What defenses does Eleanor Roosevelt give for her husband's less admirable characteristics?

3. Although she is modest, what evidence does Eleanor Roosevelt provide that reveals her great influence in Franklin Roosevelt's administration?

4. Even though she is much admired today, many people of the day were very critical of Eleanor Roosevelt. Why do you think she was so controversial?

A Terrible Responsibility

INTERVIEW WITH
PRESIDENT HARRY S TRUMAN

*Democrat Harry S Truman, President from 1945 to 1953, was
known for his homespun humor and his blunt conversational
style. In this excerpt from a 1946 interview, Truman answers questions about being the President and describes his view of necessary
presidential qualities. In the process he demonstrates his own
considerable grasp of politics and history.*

I asked President Truman if he had ever dreamed of
being President of the United States, since that seemed
to be the dream of every American boy.

He said:

"Never. No, never. I was never an **egoist**.[1] But, as
u know, I studied the lives of great men and famous

---

egoist—self-advancer.

women; and I found that the men and women who got to the top were those who did the jobs they had in hand, with everything they had of energy and enthusiasm and hard work.

"I had no idea that the lightning would ever strike me, as it has.

"The presidency of the United States is a terrible responsibility for one man. Luckily, the ten years I spent in the Senate gave me some idea and background of what to expect."

I asked him if he would talk about the problems of the presidency, just what the President faces as a man.

He said:

"The President has an executive job that is almost fantastic. There has never been one like it. I think no absolute monarch has ever had such decisions to make or the responsibility that the President of the United States has. It is really fantastic. That may not be a good word to use in regard to the presidency, but after all, every final important decision has to be made right here on the President's desk, and only the President can make it. Nobody else can do it for him, and his decisions affect millions not only in his own country but around the world. As you see, I need the best information and advice that I can get. I believe honest men will arrive at honest decisions if they have the facts."

I asked, "Can any one man alone today handle the work of the presidency?"

He replied:

"No one man really can fill the presidency. The presidency has too many and too great responsibilities. All a man can do is to try to meet them. He must be able to judge men, delegate responsibility and back up those he trusts."

"And he must have courage?" I asked.

He said:

"Well, yes. But if a President knows what the implications are of any action he takes, he will be better able to act, and he will be forthright. You must know the historical background of what makes the world go round. After all, there is little real change in the problems of government from the beginnings of time down to the present. Those problems today are just about the same as they were for Mesopotamia² and Egypt, for the Hittites,³ for Greece and Rome, for Carthage and Great Britain and France.

"The one great difference between the problems of governing in ancient and earlier days and today is that the people whom the ancients used to call "down below," the people who today exercise the real **sovereignty**,⁴ are better acquainted with what government means, and with what the purpose of government is.

"You know, government is an **intangible**⁵ thing. You hear people talk about the powers of the President. In the long run, his powers depend a good deal on his success in public relations. The President must try to get people to do the things that will be best for the most people in the country. I often say that I sit here at the President's desk talking to people and kissing them on

---

² Mesopotamia—ancient kingdom located in the present nation of Iraq. Two of the earliest human civilizations developed in Mesopotamia and Egypt.

³ Hittites—residents of an ancient country in what is now Turkey.

⁴ **sovereignty**—power and authority in government.

⁵ **intangible**—difficult to perceive or touch.

both cheeks trying to get them to do what they ought to do without getting kissed.

"The President of the United States represents 154,000,000 people. Most of them have no lobby and no special representation. The President must represent all the people.

"Therefore, the President must be a sort of super-public relations man. His powers are great, but he must know how to make people get along together. The President spends a great deal of his time trying to make people get along together. His ceremonial duties, which are incidental to his official duties, are all part of his public relations duties.

"Some people think that public relations should be based on polls. That is nonsense.

"I wonder how far Moses would have gone if he had taken a poll in Egypt?

"What would Jesus Christ have preached if He had taken a poll in the land of Israel?

"Where would the Reformation have gone if Martin Luther had taken a poll?

"It isn't polls or public opinion alone of the moment that counts. It is right and wrong, and leadership—men with **fortitude**,[6] honesty and a belief in the right that make **epochs**[7] in the history of the world.

"Today the responsibility of the President is greater than ever. The President has to know what takes place all around the world. He has to have all sorts of world contacts. Because today we are, whether we like it or not, the most powerful nation in the world.

"I think this is the most remarkable Republic in the history of the world."

---

[6] **fortitude**—courage.

[7] **epochs**—periods of history.

The President got up from his desk to point at a globe. He continued:

"This Republic has grown from a handful of colonies, right along here, with three million in population, to 154 million, with a national income of 272 billion dollars and a national production of 329 billion dollars. Those are the latest figures I have in the economic report right here.

"And it is amazing. Our appropriation for military business this year is greater than the national income of Great Britain. And so we have to assume the responsibility that we never thought we would have to assume, and which we tried to dodge for thirty years and which got us into another war. We just can't dodge that responsibility now.

"And the way to keep our economy on an even keel and keep it expanding is to encourage and help the development of the rest of the world.

"There will come a time when many of the things we need we will have to get from outside of the United States. We have to go to Labrador and to Liberia to get the ore necessary to keep our steel plants running. We have to go abroad for the copper we need. We have got copper in Arizona and Utah, but we can't get along without the copper of Chile. And there is tin in Bolivia and Malaya and rubber in Indonesia and, of course, I could add to the list of the things that we need from other parts of the world.

"As a matter of fact, we have got to interest ourselves in people of other countries, giving them a proper return for the production of the things we need, so that we can keep our own great production program going. That is the only way it can be kept going—it can't be done any other way. We can expand only if the world expands and that is why the President today has to know what is going on around the world and that is why he has greater responsibility. Because without knowing what is going on around the world he cannot exercise his judgment for his own country."

QUESTIONS TO CONSIDER

1. What qualifications did Truman have for the presidency? In what ways did he feel challenged by the job?

2. According to Truman, what qualities must a President have in order to do his job well?

3. What special challenges did Truman face as President in the late 1940s?

4. What events in the present day demonstrate the truth of Truman's words?

The Constitution and Impeachment

BY DALE BUMPERS

Near the end of the impeachment proceedings against President Bill Clinton in 1999, Dale Bumpers, a former Democratic senator from Arkansas, defended the President in a speech to the Senate. Bumpers had known and liked Clinton for a very long time. In fact, they had each earlier held the position of governor of Arkansas. In his remarks in the Senate, Bumpers considers the meaning of presidential "character" and its implications for the impeachment process.

. . . Colleagues, I come here with some sense of reluctance.

The President and I have been close friends for 25 years. We've fought so many battles back home together in our beloved Arkansas, we tried mightily all of my years as governor and his, and all of my years in the Senate when he was governor, to raise the living standards in the Delta area of Mississippi, Arkansas and Louisiana where poverty is unspeakable, with some measure of success—not nearly enough. We tried to provide health care for the lesser among us, for those who are well off enough they can't get on welfare, but not making enough to buy health insurance. . . .

The President and I have been together hundreds of times—at parades, dedications, political events, social events. And in all of those years, and all those hundreds of times we've been together, both in public and in private, I have never one time seen the President conduct himself in a way that did not reflect the highest credit on him, his family, his state, and his beloved nation.

The reason I came here today with some reluctance (please don't **misconstrue**[1] that), it has nothing to do with my feelings about the president, as I've already said, but it's because we are from the same state and we are long-time friends and I know that that necessarily diminishes to some extent the effectiveness of my words.

So if Bill Clinton the man, Bill Clinton the friend, were the issue here, I'm quite sure I would not be doing this. But it is the weight of history on all of us and it is my reverence for that great document—you heard me rail about it for 24 years—that we call our Constitution, the most sacred document to me next to the holy Bible.

These proceedings go right to the heart of our Constitution where it deals with impeachment—the part that provides the gravest punishment for just about anybody, the President—even though the framers said we're putting this in to protect the public, not to punish the President.

Ah, colleagues, you have such an awesome responsibility. My good friend, the senior senator from New York, has said it well. He says this: A decision to convict holds the potential for **destabilizing**[2] the office of the presidency. . . .

---

[1] **misconstrue**—misunderstand.
[2] **destabilizing**—making unstable.

Well, colleagues, I have heard so many adjectives to describe this gathering and these proceedings. *Historic, memorable, unprecedented, awesome*—all of those words, all of those descriptions are apt. And to those I would add the word *dangerous*—dangerous not only for the reasons I just stated, but because it's dangerous to the political process and it's dangerous to the unique mix of pure democracy and republican government Madison and his colleagues so brilliantly crafted, and which has sustained us for 210 years.

Mr. Chief Justice,[3] this is what we lawyers call "dicta." This costs you nothing. It's extra. But the more I study that document [the Constitution] and those four months in Philadelphia in 1787, the more awed I am. And you know what Madison did? The brilliance was in its simplicity. He simply said: Man's nature is to get other people to dance to their tune. Man's nature is to abuse his fellow man sometimes. And he said, the way to make sure that the majorities don't abuse the minorities, and the way to make sure that the bullies don't run over the weaklings, is to provide the same rights for everybody.

And I had to think about that a long time before I delivered my first lecture at the University of Arkansas last week. And it made so much sense to me. But the danger, as I say, is to the political process, and dangerous for reasons feared by the framers about legislative control of the executive. That single issue and how to deal with impeachment was debated off and on for the entire four months of the constitutional convention.

But the word *dangerous* is not mine. It's Alexander Hamilton's. A brilliant, good-looking guy. Mr. Ruff[4]

[3] Mr. Chief Justice—William Rehnquist. As set out in the Constitution, the chief justice of the Supreme Court presides in the Senate during impeachment trials.

[4] Mr. Ruff—Charles Ruff, President Clinton's lawyer.

quoted extensively on Tuesday afternoon in his brilliant statement here. He quoted Alexander Hamilton precisely, and it's a little **arcane**.[5] It isn't easy to understand. So if I may, at the expense of being slightly repetitious, let me paraphrase what Hamilton said. He said the Senate had a unique role in participating with the executive branch in appointment. And two, it had a role—it had a role in participating with the executive in the character of a court for the trial of impeachments. But he said—and I must say this, and you all know it—he said it would be difficult to get what he called a well-constituted court from wholly elected members. He said passions would agitate the whole community and divide it between those who were friendly and those who had **inimical**[6] interest to the accused, namely the President. And then he said, and these are his words, the greatest danger was that the decision would be based on the comparative strength of the parties rather than the innocence or guilt of the President.

You have a solemn oath. You have taken a solemn oath to be fair and impartial. I know you all, I know you as friends, and I know you as honorable men, and I'm perfectly satisfied to put that in your hands under your oath. This is the only **caustic**[7] thing I will say in these remarks this afternoon, but the question is, "How did we come to be here?" We are here because of a five-year relentless, unending investigation of the President.

Fifty million dollars, hundreds of FBI agents fanning across the nation examining in detail the microscopic lives of people, maybe the most intense investigation not only of a President but of anybody, ever. I feel this strongly just because of my state and

---

[5] **arcane**—complex and possibly outdated.

[6] **inimical**—hostile.

[7] **caustic**—cutting; biting.

what we have endured. So you'll have to excuse me, but that investigation has also shown that the judicial system in this country can and does get out of kilter unless it's controlled. Because there are innocent people—innocent people who have been financially and mentally bankrupted. . . .

You're here today because the President suffered a terrible moral lapse, a marital infidelity. Not a breach of the public trust, not a crime against society, the two things Hamilton talked about in *Federalist Paper No. 65*— I recommend it to you before you vote. But it was a breach of his marriage vows. It was a breach of his family trust. It is a sex scandal. [Journalist] H.L. Mencken said one time, "When you hear somebody say, 'This is not about money,' it's about money." And when you hear somebody say, 'This is not about sex,' it's about sex. You pick your own adjective to describe the President's conduct. Here are some that I would use: indefensible, outrageous, unforgivable, shameless. I promise you the President would not contest any of those or any others.

But there's a human element in this case that has not even been mentioned, and that is the President and Hillary and Chelsea[8] are human beings. This is intended only as a mild criticism of our distinguished friends in the House, but as I listened to the presenters, to the managers[9] make their opening statements, they were remarkably well-prepared, and they spoke eloquently, more eloquent than I really had hoped. But when I talk about the human element, I talk about what I thought was, on occasion, unnecessarily harsh and **pejorative**[10] descriptions of the President. I thought that language should have been tempered somewhat, to acknowledge

---

[8] Hillary and Chelsea—President Clinton's wife and daughter.

[9] managers—the members of the House of Representatives that managed the impeachment investigation and brought the case against Clinton to the Senate.

[10] **pejorative**—critical; demeaning.

that he is the President. To say constantly that the President lied about this and lied about that, as I say, I thought that was too much for a family that has already been about as decimated as a family can get.

The relationship between husband and wife, father and child has been incredibly strained, if not destroyed. There's been nothing but sleepless nights, mental agony for this family for almost five years. Day after day, from accusations of having assassinated, or had Vince Foster[11] assassinated on down. It has been bizarre.

But I didn't sense any compassion, and perhaps none is deserved. The President has said for all to hear that he misled, he deceived, he did not want to be helpful to the prosecution. And he did all of those things to his family, to his friends, to his staff, to his cabinet and to the American people. Why would he do that? Well, he knew this whole affair was about to bring unspeakable embarrassment and humiliation on himself, his wife whom he adored, and a child that he worshipped with every fiber in his body, and for whom he would happily have died to spare her this or to **ameliorate**[12] her shame and her grief.

The House managers have said shame and embarrassment is no excuse for lying. Well, the question about lying, that's your decision. But I can tell you, you put yourself in his position, and you've already had this big moral lapse, as to what you would do. We are none of us perfect. Sure, you say, he should have thought of all that beforehand. And indeed he should. Just as Adam and Eve should have.

Just as you and you and you and you, and millions of other people who have been caught in similar circumstances, should have thought of it before. And I say, none of us are perfect.

---

[11] Vince Foster—a Clinton aide whose suicide prevented investigators from questioning him.

[12] **ameliorate**—moderate; soften.

I remember, Chaplain [the Senate clergyman who offers prayers at their sessions], the—the Chaplain's not here, is he? That's too bad. He ought to hear this story. This evangelist was holding this great revival meeting, and at the close of one of his meetings, he said, "Is there anybody in this audience who has ever known anybody who even comes close to the perfection of our Lord and Savior, Jesus Christ?" Nothing. He repeated the challenge, and finally a itty bitty guy in the back of the audience kind of held up his hand, and he said, "You. Are you saying you've known such a person? Stand up."

He stood up, and he said, "Tell us, share it with us. Who was it?"

He said, "My wife's first husband."

Make no mistake about it, removal from office is punishment, it is unbelievable punishment, even though the framers didn't quite see it that way.

Again they said, and it bears repeating over and over again, they said they wanted to protect the people. But I can tell you this: The punishment of removing Bill Clinton from office would pale compared to the punishment he has already inflicted on himself.

There's a feeling in this country that somehow or other Bill Clinton's gotten away with something. Mr. Leader, I can tell you, he hasn't gotten away with anything. And the people are saying, "Please don't protect us from this man, 76 percent of us think he's doing a fine job; 65 percent of us don't want him removed from office."[13] . . .

Impeachment was debated off and on in Philadelphia for the entire four months [of the deliberations of the Constitutional Convention of 1787], as I said. The key

---

[13] Bumpers is referring to public opinion polls that showed that a majority of the American people believed Clinton should not be removed from office.

players were Gouverneur Morris, . . . a brilliant Pennsylvanian.

George Mason, the only man reputedly to have been so brilliant that Thomas Jefferson actually deferred to him. And he [Mason] refused to sign the Constitution, incidentally, even though he was a delegate, because they didn't deal with slavery and he was a strict abolitionist.

And then there was Charles Pinkney. . . from South Carolina, just a youngster, 29 years old, I believe.

Edmund Randolph from Virginia, who had a big role in the Constitution in the beginning—the Virginia Plan. And then there was, of course, James Madison, the craftsman.

They were all key players in drafting this impeachment provision. And uppermost in the mind during the entire time they were composing was they did not want any kings. They had lived under **despots**,[14] they had lived under kings, they had lived under **autocrats**,[15] and they didn't want any of that. And they succeeded very admirably. We've had 46 presidents[16] and no kings.

But they kept talking about corruption, maybe that ought to be the reason for impeachment, because they feared some president would corrupt the political process (that's what the debate was about) corrupt the political process and **ensconce**[17] himself through a phony election, maybe as something close to a king.

They followed the British rule on impeachment, because the British said the House of Commons may impeach and the House of Lords must convict. And every one of the colonies had the same procedure: House, Senate. Though, in all fairness, House members,

---

[14] **despots**—cruel rulers.

[15] **autocrats**—absolute rulers.

[16] Bumpers is mistaken here. At that time, there had been 41 Presidents.

[17] **ensconce**—to securely settle in.

Alexander Hamilton was not very keen on the House participating.

But here was the sequence of events at Philadelphia that brought us here today. They started out with "maladministration," and Madison said that's too vague. What does that mean? So they dropped that. They went from that to "corruption" and they dropped that. Then they went to "malpractice." And they decided that was not definitive enough.

And they went to "treason, bribery and corruption." And they decided that still didn't suit them. But bear in mind one thing. During this entire process, they are narrowing—they are narrowing the things you can impeach the President for. They were making it tougher. Madison said if we aren't careful, the President will serve at the pleasure of the legislature—the Senate—he said.

And then they went to "treason and bribery" and somebody said that's still not quite enough.

And so they went to treason, bribery, and, George Mason added, "or other high crimes and misdemeanors against the United States." And they voted on it, and on Sept. 10 they sent the entire Constitution to a committee.

They called a committee on style and arrangement, which was the committee that would draft the language in a way that everybody would understand; it would be well-crafted from a grammatical standpoint. But that committee, which was dominated by Madison and Hamilton, dropped "against the United States." And historians will tell you that the reason they did that was because of **redundance**,[18] because that committee had no right to change the substance of anything. They would not have dropped it if they hadn't felt that it was redundant.

---

[18] **redundance**—repetition; having been previously established.

And then, they put in for good measure—we can always be grateful—the two-thirds majority.

Now this is one of the most important points of this entire presentation: The term, first of all, "treason and bribery," nobody quarrels with that, (and we're not debating treason and bribery here in this chamber) we're talking about "other high crimes and misdemeanors."

And where did "high crimes and misdemeanors" come from? It came from the English law, and they found it in an English law under a category which said, "distinctly political offenses against the state." Let me repeat that. They said "high crimes and misdemeanors" was to be (because they took it from English law) where they found it in the category that said, "offenses distinctly political against the state."

So colleagues, please, for just one moment, forget the complexities of the facts and the tortured legalisms. And we've heard them all brilliantly presented on both sides, and I'm not getting into that. But ponder this. If "high crimes and misdemeanors" was taken from English law by George Mason, which listed high crimes and misdemeanors as political offenses against the state, what are we doing here?

If, as Hamilton said, it had to be a crime against society or a breach of the public trust, what are we doing here?

Even perjury, concealing or deceiving an unfaithful relationship, does not even come close to being an impeachable offense.

Nobody has suggested that Bill Clinton committed a political crime against the state. So, colleagues, if you honor the Constitution, you must look at the history of the Constitution and how we got to the impeachment clause. And if you do that and you do that honestly, according to the oath you took, you cannot—you can censure Bill Clinton, you can hand him over to the prosecutor for him to be prosecuted—but you cannot convict him. And you cannot indulge yourselves the luxury or the right to ignore this history.

... my love for that document [the Constitution] came day after day in debate after debate right here in this chamber. . . .

And the reason I developed this love of it is because I saw Madison's magic working time and time again, keeping bullies from running over weak people, keeping majorities from running over minorities. And I thought about all the unfettered freedoms we had. The oldest organic law in existence made us the envy of the world.

Mr. Chairman, we've also learned that the rule of law includes presidential elections. That's a part of the rule of law in this country. We have an event, a **quadrennial**[19] event in this country, which we call "presidential elections." And that's the day when we reach across this aisle and hold hands, Democrats and Republicans. And we say, "Win or lose, we will abide by the decision."

It is a solemn event, presidential elections, and it should not—they should not—be undone lightly. Or just because one side has the clout and the other one doesn't.

The American people are now, and for some time have been asking, to be allowed a good night's sleep. They're asking for an end to this nightmare. It is a legitimate request.

I'm not suggesting that you vote for or against the polls. I understand that. Nobody should vote against the polls just to show their **mettle**[20] and their courage. I have cast plenty of votes against the polls and it's cost

---

[19] **quadrennial**—every four years.

[20] **mettle**—spirit; character.

me politically a lot of times. This has been going on for a year, though.

And in [an article he wrote for a newspaper] I talked about meeting Harry Truman [during] my first year as governor of Arkansas. Spent an hour with him. An **indelible**[21] experience. People at home kid me about this, because I very seldom make a speech that I don't mention this meeting. But I will never forget what he said, "Put your faith in the people. Trust the people. They can handle it."

They have shown conclusively time and time again that they can handle it.

Colleagues, this is easily the most important vote you will ever cast. If you have difficulty because of an intense dislike of the President—and that's understandable—rise above it. He is not the issue.

He will be gone. You won't. So don't leave a precedent from which we may never recover and almost surely will regret.

If you vote to acquit, Mr. Leader, you know exactly what's going to happen. You're going back to your committees, you're going to get on this legislative agenda, you're going to start dealing with Medicare and Social Security and tax cuts and all those things which the people of the country have a nonnegotiable demand that you do.

If you vote to acquit, you go immediately to the people's agenda. But if you vote to convict, you can't be sure what's going to happen. James G. Blaine was a member of the Senate when Andrew Johnson was tried in 1868, and 20 years later he **recanted**.[22] And he said: "I made a bad mistake." And he says, "As I reflect back on it, all I can think about is having convicted Andrew Johnson would have caused much more chaos and

---

[21] **indelible**—unforgettable.

[22] **recanted**—renounced.

confusion in this country than Andrew Johnson could ever conceivably have tried."

And so it is with William Jefferson Clinton. If you vote to convict, in my opinion you're going to be creating [more] havoc than he could ever possibly create. After all, he's only got two years left. So don't, for God's sake, heighten people's **alienation**,[23] that is at an all-time high, toward their government.

The people have a right and they are calling on you to rise above politics, rise above partisanship. They're calling on you to do your solemn duty. And I pray you will.

Thank you, Mr. Chief Justice.

---

[23] **alienation**—withdrawal; estrangement.

QUESTIONS TO CONSIDER

1. What does Bumpers mean by the statement that "A decision to convict holds the potential for destabilizing the office of the presidency"?

2. How does the author use the *Federalist Paper No. 65* to argue that Clinton did not commit impeachable acts?

3. What argument, based on the debate at the Constitutional Convention, does Bumpers use to support his view?

4. To what extent is high moral character a requirement of a successful President? Has this aspect of the presidency changed since Washington's time?

The Ultimate Approval Rating

BY ARTHUR M. SCHLESINGER, JR.

Schlesinger—a prominent historian, biographer and aide to President John Kennedy (1961–1963)—has continued a poll begun by his father in which historians give report cards to all the Presidents. They also assess the personal qualities and abilities necessary to be rated among the "great" Presidents in United States history.

The game of ranking Presidents is a popular pastime among scholars. My father, Arthur M. Schlesinger, for 40 years a professor at Harvard and a more eminent historian than his son, started it all nearly half a century ago. In 1948 he invited 55 leading historians to render their verdicts. The scholars' ratings, published in *Life* magazine just before Truman confounded the prophets and won reelection, excited interest and controversy. In 1962 *The Times Magazine* prevailed upon my father to repeat the poll. Again much interest and much controversy.

The Schlesinger polls asked historians to place each President (omitting W. H. Harrison and Garfield because they died so soon after taking office) in one of five categories: Great, Near Great, Average, Below Average and Failure. The standard was not lifetime achievement but performance in the White House. The scholars were to decide for themselves how Presidential performance was to be judged. It was supposed that historians would know greatness—or failure—when they saw it, as Justice Potter Stewart famously said of pornography.

Presidents might well have wondered (and some did): Who are historians to **arrogate**[1] to themselves the judging of Presidential performance? The Presidential office, said Calvin Coolidge in an **unwonted**[2] lyrical outburst, "remains a great mystery. . . .Like the glory of a morning sunrise, it can only be experienced—it cannot be told." John F. Kennedy said to me: "How the hell can you tell? Only the President himself can know what his real pressures and real alternatives are. If you don't know that, how can you judge performance?" Some of his greatest predecessors, he continued, received credit for doing things when they could have done nothing else; only detailed inquiry could disclose what difference Presidents made by their individual contributions. War, he observed, made it easier for a President to achieve greatness. But would Lincoln have been judged so great a President if he had had to face the almost **insoluble**[3] problem of Reconstruction?

Many polls have been taken, and there have been nine Greats and Near Greats in nearly all the reckonings. Lincoln, Washington and Franklin D. Roosevelt are always at the top, followed, in varying order, by Jefferson, Jackson, Polk, Theodore Roosevelt, Wilson

---

[1] **arrogate**—assign.

[2] **unwonted**—rare.

[3] **insoluble**—without a solution.

and Truman. Occasionally John Adams and Cleveland join the top nine. The Failures have always been Grant and Harding, with Buchanan, Pierce, Fillmore, Taylor and Coolidge always near the bottom.

The choice of best and worst Presidents has remained relatively stable through the years. There is much fluctuation in between. Some Presidents—particularly John Quincy Adams, Buchanan, Andrew Johnson and Cleveland—have declined in later polls, but the most striking change has been the rise of Eisenhower from 22nd place in the Schlesinger 1962 poll to 12th in David Porter's 1981 poll, to 11th in the poll taken by Robert Murray and Tim Blessing in 1982 and to 9th in Steve Neal's *Chicago Tribune* poll the same year.

Over the years it has been periodically suggested that I replicate my father's polls. But the difficulty of making judgments about some of the Presidents since Eisenhower stumped me—in the cases of Kennedy and Ford, because of the brevity of their time in office; in the cases of Lyndon Johnson, Nixon and Bush, because their domestic and foreign records are so **discordant**.[4] Scholars might be inclined to rate Johnson higher in domestic than in foreign affairs and do the reverse for Nixon and Bush. And the most recent Presidents always seem more controversial. Still, the passage of time encourages new perspectives. So in 1996 *The Times Magazine* took a new poll.

The question of **disjunction**[5] still nags in the cases of Johnson, Nixon and Bush. "I find three cases which one could describe as having **dichotomous**[6] or **schizoid**[7] profiles," Walter Dean Burnham says. "On some very important dimensions, both Wilson and L.B. Johnson were outright failures in my view while on others they

---

[4] **discordant**—conflicting.
[5] **disjunction**—division.
[6] **dichotomous**—two-sided.
[7] **schizoid**—split.

rank very high indeed. Similarly with Nixon. . . ." Alan Brinkley says, "There are Presidents who could be considered *both* failures *and* great or near great (e.g. Wilson, Johnson, Nixon)." James MacGregor Burns observed of Nixon: How can one evaluate such an **idiosyncratic**[8] President, so brilliant and so morally lacking? . . . So I guess to average out he would be average."

Yet the 1996 poll still shows a high degree of scholarly consensus. Lincoln, with a unanimous Great vote, comes in first in 1996. Washington and F.D.R., as usual, are next; each had one Near Great vote. The big three are followed, as usual, by the Near Greats—Jefferson, Jackson, Polk, Theodore Roosevelt, Wilson and Truman.

Most Presidents fall in the Average class. Recent Presidents, too close for the cool eye of history, are most likely to rise or fall in polls to come. Carter currently has one Near Great and two Failures, with the rest of his votes in between. Some admire his accomplishment in putting human rights on the world's agenda; others deplore his political ineptitude and the absence of any clear direction in his handling of domestic affairs.

Reagan, on the other hand, has seven Near Great votes, including some from liberal scholars impressed by his success in restoring the prestige of the Presidency, in negotiating the last phases of the Cold War and in imposing his priorities on the country. But he also receives nine Below Averages and four Failures from those who consider his priorities—his attack on government and his tax reductions that increased **disparities**[9] between rich and poor while tripling the national debt—a disaster for the Republic.

Reagan's score actually comes out a shade below that of Bush, who receives no Near Greats but more Averages than Reagan and only one Failure. Bush's skill

---

[8] **idiosyncratic**—peculiar; eccentric.

[9] **disparities**—differences.

in putting together the coalition that won the Gulf War outweighs for many his seeming lack of purpose in domestic policy.

The list of failures shows a slight shift from past polls. Harding and Grant are, as usual, favorite Failures. Do they really deserve it? They are marked down because of the scandal and corruption that disgraced their Administrations. But they were careless rather than villainous. Their sin was excessive loyalty to crooked friends. "Harding was not a bad man," as Theodore Roosevelt's daughter, Alice Roosevelt Longworth, put it. "He was just a slob." Scandal and corruption are indefensible, but they may injure the general welfare less than misconceived policies.

The belated national sensitivity to racial injustice may explain why two Presidents receive more Failure votes this time than in earlier polls: James Buchanan, whose **irresolution**[10] encouraged the secession of the Confederate states; and Andrew Johnson, who, while a Unionist, was a **stout**[11] believer in white supremacy. It seems reasonable to suggest that Buchanan, Andrew Johnson, Hoover and Nixon—the one President who resigned to escape impeachment—damaged the Republic more than did the hapless Grant and the feckless Harding.

Nine men, we have seen, continue to lead the list as they did in the first Schlesinger poll. What do Washington, Jefferson, Jackson, Polk, Lincoln, Theodore Roosevelt, Wilson, Franklin Roosevelt and Truman have in common? What do they tell us about the qualities necessary for success in the White House?

Intelligence is helpful, though Reagan—with seven Near Greats—showed that an influential President need not have much. Maturity? The British ambassador

---

[10] **irresolution**—inability to make up his mind.
[11] **stout**—strong.

thought Theodore Roosevelt was an arrested 11-year-old. Loyalty? This can be a Presidential defect: remember Grant and Harding. Private virtues do not guarantee public effectiveness.

More to the point is the test proposed 125 years ago by our most brilliant historian, Henry Adams. The American President, he wrote, "resembles the commander of a ship at sea. He must have a helm to grasp, a course to steer, a port to seek." The course and the port constitute the first requirement for Presidential greatness. Great Presidents possess, or are possessed by, a vision of an ideal America. Their passion is to make sure the ship of state sails on the right course.

If that course is indeed right, it is because they have an instinct for the dynamics of history. "A statesman may be determined and **tenacious**,"[12] de Gaulle said, "but if he does not understand the character of his time, he will fail." Great Presidents have a deep connection with the needs, anxieties, and dreams of the people. "I do not believe," said Wilson, "that any man can lead who does not act . . . under the impulse of a profound sympathy with those whom he leads."

Franklin Roosevelt said that our Great Presidents were "leaders of thought at times when certain ideas in the life of the nation had to be clarified." So Washington **embodied**[13] the idea of the Federal union, Jefferson and Jackson the idea of democracy, Lincoln union and freedom, Cleveland rugged honesty. Theodore Roosevelt and Wilson, said F.D.R., were both "moral leaders, each in his own way and his own time, who used the Presidency as a pulpit."

To succeed, Presidents must have a port to seek and must convince Congress and the electorate of the rightness of their course. Politics in a democracy is ultimately

---

[12] **tenacious**—tough.

[13] **embodied**—symbolized.

an educational process, an exercise in persuasion and consent. Every President stands in Theodore Roosevelt's "bully pulpit." National crisis widens his range of options but does not automatically make the man. The crisis of rebellion did not spur Buchanan to greatness, nor did the Depression turn Hoover into a bold and imaginative leader. Their inadequacies in the face of crisis allowed Lincoln and the second Roosevelt to show the difference that individuals can make to history.

Some of the top nine made their mark without benefit of first-order crisis. Presidents like Jackson and Theodore Roosevelt forced the nation through sheer power of personality to recognize **incipient**[14] problems— Jackson in vindicating the national authority against the Bank of the United States; the first Roosevelt in vindicating the national authority against the great corporations. As the historian Elting Morison described this quality of noncrisis leadership: "Theodore Roosevelt could get the attention of his fellow citizens and make them think—He knew . . . how to startle the country into informing debate; and how to move people into their thinking beyond short-run self-interest toward some longer view of the general welfare."

We hear much these days about the virtues of the middle of the road. Bur none of the top nine can be described as a middle-roader. Middle-roading may be fine for campaigning but it is a sure road to **mediocrity**[15] in governing. The middle of the road is not the vital center: it is the dead center. Clinton would be wise to eschew it if he wants to improve his ratings. The Greats and the Near Greats all took risks in pursuit of their ideals. They all provoked intense controversy. They all, except Washington, divided the nation before reuniting it on a new level of national understanding.

---

[14] **incipient**—beginning.

[15] **mediocrity**—nonaccomplishment

Every President would like to be loved by everyone in the country, but Presidents who sacrifice convictions to a quest for affection are unlikely to make it to the top. Harding was an immensely popular President. His death provoked an outpouring of national grief that observers thought unmatched since the death of Lincoln. Yet scholars are unanimous in pronouncing him a Failure.

Presidents who seek to change the nation's direction know they will alienate those who profit from the status quo. Great Presidents go ahead anyway. "Judge me," F.D.R. said, "by the enemies I've made." Truman's approval rating at the end of his Presidency was down to 31 percent. Look where he ranks now.

The 1996 Tally

Great
Washington
Lincoln
F.D. Roosevelt

Near Great
Jefferson
Jackson
Polk
T. Roosevelt
Wilson
Truman

High Average
Monroe
Cleveland
McKinley
Eisenhower
Kennedy
L.B. Johnson

Low Average
Arthur
B. Harrison
Taft
Ford
Carter
Reagan
Bush
Clinton

Below Average
Tyler
Taylor
Fillmore
Coolidge

Failure
Pierce
Buchanan
A. Johnson
Grant
Harding
Hoover
Nixon

QUESTIONS TO CONSIDER

1. What procedures have historians followed in "the game of ranking Presidents"? How effective are these procedures, and how useful is the game?

2. What difficulties in rating recent Presidents does the author cite?

3. What are the reasons Presidents have been ranked as failures?

4. What characteristics appear to be common to those ranked as "great"? Which characteristics do you think are most important for "great" Presidents? Explain.

ACKNOWLEDGEMENTS

Texts

10 From "Benjamin Franklin and Executive Pay" in *The Shaping of America* by Page Smith, McGraw-Hill, 1980, p. 67.

31 "Dorothy Thompson Dissents," *Washington Star*, Feb. 10, 1937, quoted in *Congressional Digest*, XVI, 96 (March 1937).

35 Reprinted with the permission of Simon & Schuster, from *Shadow* by Bob Woodward. Copyright © 1999 by Bob Woodward.

66 From *The Powers That Be* by David Halberstam. Copyright © 1975, 1976, 1977, 1979 by David Halberstam. Reprinted by permission of Alfred A. Knopf, a Division of Random House, Inc.

100 From *Jesse Jackson & The Politics of Race*, Thomas H. Landess and Richard M. Quinn, Jameson Books, 1985.

139 From *Eisenhower and the Cold War* by Robert Divine. Copyright © 1981 by Robert Divine. Used by permission of Oxford University Press.

153 From *Lyndon Johnson and the American Dream* by Doris Kearns. Copyright © 1976 by Doris Kearns. Reprinted by permission of HarperCollins Publishers, Inc.

170 From James David Barber, *The Presidential Character*, Prentice-Hall, Inc., © 1972, 1977, 1985, James David Barber.

201 From *This I Remember* by Eleanor Roosevelt, Harper & Brothers, 1949.

210 Excerpt from *Mr. President: The First Publication from The Personal Diaries, Private Letters, Papers and Revealing Interviews of Harry S. Truman* by William Hillman. Copyright © 1952 by William Hillman. Copyright renewed 1980 by William Hillman, Jr. Reprinted by permission of Farrar, Straus and Giroux, LLC.

Images

Photo Research Diane Hamilton.

57–61, 63 *top*, **104–107, 110–111, 161–164, 166, 168** *top*, **195–200** Courtesy Library of Congress.

108–109, 112, 165, 167 Courtesy National Archives.

62–63 *bottom*, **64, 113** © Washington Post; Reprinted by permission of the D.C. Public Library.

114 © Quest-France/Liaison Agency.

115 © Richard Faverty/Liaison Agency.

116 © Dirck Halstead/Liaison Agency.

168 *bottom* © White House/Liaison Agency.

All other photos courtesy of the Library of Congress and the National Archives.

Every effort has been made to secure complete rights and permissions for each selection presented herein. Updated acknowledgments, if needed, will appear in subsequent printings.

Index